Selling
the
Dream

Selling

the

Dream

THE
BILLION-DOLLAR
INDUSTRY
BANKRUPTING AMERICANS

Jane Marie

ATRIA BOOKS

New York   London   Toronto   Sydney   New Delhi

ATRIA
BOOKS

An Imprint of Simon & Schuster, LLC
1230 Avenue of the Americas
New York, NY 10020

Copyright © 2024 by Jane Marie

First Atria Books hardcover edition March 2024

ATRIA BOOKS and colophon are trademarks of Simon & Schuster, LLC.

Simon & Schuster: Celebrating 100 Years of Publishing in 2024

For information about special discounts for bulk purchases,
please contact Simon & Schuster Special Sales at
1-866-506-1949 or business@simonandschuster.com.

The Simon & Schuster Speakers Bureau can bring authors to your live event. For more information or to book an event, contact the Simon & Schuster Speakers Bureau at 1-866-248-3049 or visit our website at www.simonspeakers.com.

Interior design by Jill Putorti

Manufactured in the United States of America

1 3 5 7 9 10 8 6 4 2

Library of Congress Cataloging-in-Publication Data
Name: Marie, Jane (Journalist), author.
Title: Selling the dream : the billion-dollar industry bankrupting Americans / by Jane Marie.
Description: First Atria books hardcover edition. | New York : Atria Books, 2024. | Includes bibliographical references and index.
Identifiers: LCCN 2023035155 (print) | LCCN 2023035156 (ebook) | ISBN 9781982155773 (hardcover) | ISBN 9781982155780 (trade paperback) | ISBN 9781982155797 (ebook)
Subjects: LCSH: Multilevel marketing—United States. | Swindlers and swindling—United States. | Working class—United States—Economic conditions.
Classification: LCC HF5415.126 .M37 2024 (print) | LCC HF5415.126 (ebook) | DDC 658.8/72—dc23/eng/20230913
LC record available at https://lccn.loc.gov/2023035155
LC ebook record available at https://lccn.loc.gov/2023035156

ISBN 978-1-9821-5577-3
ISBN 978-1-9821-5579-7 (ebook)

For Maxine

Contents

Selling
the
Dream

Introduction

It has, at times, sounded tempting . . . even to me.

There was the night in 1996 when I was eighteen, unemployed for the first time in four years and trying to finish up high school after dropping out my junior year. I had moved back in with my dad in middle-of-nowhere Michigan after a rough turn living in a punk house in Ann Arbor. Now that I was back on the farm, I had few friends and no income. But I *did* have my own room and a TV/VCR combo with cable, and if I jiggled the coax pin just right, I could get some pretty decent soft-core porn to come through when I had trouble sleeping, which was always. If the porn trick didn't work, the other option was infomercials. On this lonely, late school night, the half-hour infomercial I landed on was for an instructional course on selling merchandise through advertising in the backs of magazines. I was mesmerized.

Remember those little two-by-two-inch ads in *Seventeen* or *Reader's Digest* for drawing classes (the turtle!) or modeling school or a beautiful figurine of Dorothy from *The Wizard of Oz*? Well, this TV pitchman promised me—dropout, burn-out, eighteen-year-old, shaved-headed me—that if I bought his books and CDs, listened carefully to his words, and then called his experts, I could become an importer and distributor of literally any product in the world. And then I'd have a yacht. I had no credit card and debit cards were a new idea, so I ordered the "course" COD. It arrived a week later, paid for with money that was not mine. I remember three things about it:

1. The packaging was enormous for the piddly amount of material it held.
2. It contained a directory of Chinese manufacturers who would cook up any tchotchke you could imagine.
3. There were dozens of sign-up sheets for "friends and family" who might want to explore this opportunity themselves.

It was a pyramid scheme. I knew this right away. How I *didn't* know it at 1:00 a.m. on a weeknight after having been on drugs instead of in school for a year is pretty obvious. But I knew it once I had it in my hands in the cold light of day.

* * *

Shortly after all of this, my friend Marcy had just returned to our hometown after quitting college and wanted to get out of her parents' house, and we convinced each other that together we could live on our own, once and for all. We soon moved into a brand-new apartment complex, the fanciest apartment building our tiny town had ever seen. This two-bedroom unit came fully carpeted, with vaulted ceilings and en suite bathrooms, and best of all they accepted the applications of two mentally and monetarily unstable nineteen-year-olds for their most deluxe home, which ran us $600 a month total in 1998. It was rad.

Everyone wanted to hang out at our apartment. We had the party house, and we'd hit the jackpot as far as neighbors were concerned. The octogenarian living below us was so hard of hearing that she'd regularly ask if her canasta group was too loud the night before. We were living the high life! But we didn't have a ton of money. I was working for my half of the rent and gas money at a café my dad and I opened to "keep me off the streets." We went under fairly quickly, partly because I was an idiot child and partly because folks kept complaining that our cappuccinos were too expensive compared to the ones at the gas station across the street. For a little extra spending money, I started a side hustle as an house-interior painter specializing in faux finishes. I could match your walls to your leather couch using a special technique with paint thinner and Saran wrap. The ways in which the nineties were particularly unkind to rural America are innumerable.

You might be wondering here, "Jane, what about college?" My parents wondered the same thing. Toward the end of my tenure at the café, when I was nineteen, I started taking classes at the local community college, studying interior design. I'd miraculously gotten a merit scholarship from the state based on my ACT score, and that paid for pretty much everything. It's remarkable how spread thin and broke one can be at that age and still look at life as half-full. That was the attitude, I'm sure, that led to me being tempted by a scammer once again.

One day a mutual friend of Marcy's and mine asked if we'd be so kind as to allow her to throw a party at our glorious home. An all-girls party. An all-girls lingerie party. I practically ran to the local copy shop and made paper invites using clip art, as hardly anyone we knew had an email address. This was going to be *so* sexy. And as if making finger sandwiches for a roomful of ladies trying on boudoir sets wasn't rewarding enough, as hostesses we each got to keep a set of unmentionables for ourselves as a reward.

You know where this is going! It was a multi-level-marketing pitch disguised as a fun party. I was the perfect potential recruit at the time: young, female, living in a small town with limited employment options, outgoing, and, most insulting of all, seemingly gullible. I knew this impression of me made me seem an easy target, but I kind of didn't care. Unbeknownst to the friend throwing this "party," I wasn't looking for another job. So, I accepted the free garter belt, which was awesome, if unnecessary—there was no one to wear it for in about a fifty-mile radius and camgirl wasn't a job yet—and went on my merry way.

In hindsight, I do feel terrible that I'd roped a dozen or so of my girlfriends into attending that party, and that more than a few of them signed up to sell the stuff themselves, right there on the spot. I'm sure it seemed like a great opportunity for many of them, and had I not already been employed and overwhelmed, it would've been attractive to me as well. It always sounds like an exaggeration when I talk about how limited our options were if we stayed in that town after high school. The auto industry in Flint had kept the place afloat for half a century but was on its last legs by the time we came of age. There just wasn't much on offer in the way of money in our small rural community, so, as my grandma says, "You learn to scrape money off the walls if you can find it."

These days, opportunities to sell lingerie—or anything, really—to your friends and family while also recruiting them to be sellers aren't nearly as hard to come by, and that's what we're here to explore.

If you're anything like me, when you open Facebook or Instagram, your DMs are flooded with messages laden with emojis that resemble the following:

Hey hun! 🐿 Wow, haven't seen u since high school!! 📱 You look amazing. 👏 👏 👏 I'm reaching out cuz I need just THREE more friends to buy the most 💜 amazing 💜 mascara [insert of woefully disappointing photo of spider eyelashes of said "friend"] from this 💄 fab 🏭 company I work for to meet my monthly sales goal 💰!!! Sale ends at midnight & if you order in the next hour I'll throw in a mystery gift! 🎁

If you've ever been on the receiving end of these pitches, then you already know that if you don't reply, no worries! They'll be back with the same message next month. If you *do* reply with any answer, be it yes or no or "Go away, we are not and have never been friends," you are guaranteed to get a follow-up message that looks like some version of the following:

🙋 Well, let me know if you're ever interested in quitting you're job 😩 😩 to work for urself like I do, or if ya just wanna make a lil fun money. 💸 💸 💸 Bye hun! XOXO 💋

It's easy to roll your eyes at the above when you're reading it in a book that you know is critical of these sorts of schemes, but it's heartbreaking, to some of us, when we see our loved ones—friends, coworkers, and in my case family members— wasting so much time, energy, money, and self-worth on such scams. How is anyone saying yes? How did we get here? Well, as I've spent the last several years digging deeper than anyone should ever have to into the world of multi-level marketing, it is my distinct displeasure to tell you.

But, first, we need to define some terms.

Multi-level marketing is called a million different things depending on the angle of the person who is doing the pitching. Some might call it *direct sales*. Some use the term *network marketing*. For my own sanity and the health of my computer keyboard, I'll mostly be referring to multi-level marketing companies as MLMs.

Whatever the name, they all work in basically the same way. In a triangular-shaped business structure, the owners and very early registrants sit at the top. They then set out to recruit teams of sellers under them. There's almost always a start-up fee, which is frequently set just below the number (often $499) at which a member is defined as a franchisee and the company must follow franchise law, which requires them to publicly disclose financial information.

Information gathering and sharing is actively discouraged in most MLMs. The marketing materials used to lure prospective distributors seem carefully and purposefully written—often by teams of lawyers—to confuse yet inspire a prospect. Compensation structures are highly complex and delivered in "packets" the size of novellas where the answer to "How will I make money?" appears intentionally obscured.

That obscurity has been given a name by the Federal Trade Commission (FTC): "deceptive or unfair earnings claims." Many of these compensation packets open with paragraphs about hopes and dreams, empowerment and freedom, without a number in sight. During recruitment, bookkeeping is never spoken about; you'll be too busy rolling in money to worry about keeping a balance sheet. Are you in?

Once registrants have signed up and paid the fee, they are expected to find their own recruits using the same techniques, and those folks are expected to do the same, ad infinitum.

If you have been recruited and are not the owner of the company or at the very top, you will have what are called "uplines" and "downlines." Uplines consist of the person who recruited you and anyone above that person. Downlines are typically made up of your recruits. *Another* skeevy thing about this world: new recruits are encouraged to recruit their nearest and dearest first. After all, the most important feature of any successful business venture is *trust*, and who trusts you more than your best friend or your mom?

Most companies set a target of five recruits for each new person in the . . . triangle. This business model is phony on its face because by doing a little simple math, you can see it takes fewer than thirteen cycles of this process for *one* MLM to run out of humans on Earth to recruit.

Some MLMs purport to sell products. Take Amway, for

example. They're the company whose distributors are notorious for inviting you over to their house for a friendly dinner only to have it turn into a pitch meeting with your neighbors begging you to sell products from their giant catalog of home goods right alongside them. Amway is so famous for this that it was parodied as "Confederated Products" in the film *Go*. Amway famously started out selling soap. All-natural, extra-special soap that was somehow *only* available through an elite network of individual distributors. Soap one could only buy if one also wanted to sell it. Soap that could never, nay, *would* never be sold in grocery stores for some reason that I'm sure you find out once you've paid the sign-up fee to become an Amway distributor.

In an MLM, the product being sold doesn't matter since most of the money is being made via those recruitment fees and distributors stocking their own shelves with inventory. Companies market makeup or vitamins or diet programs or insurance or videophones. Some MLMs sell no product at all. Countless companies have cropped up in recent decades "selling" the opportunity to learn how to sell the opportunity to people who might be interested in learning how to sell the opportunity to others who may not even know they're interested in learning to sell the opportunity to learn how to sell. These folks are the ones who prefer the term *network marketing*, but the element that makes them network marketers is the *network* part: to be in the network, you must build your own network, and that network invariably ends up looking like a big old triangle with the guy doing the talking on top.

It's plainly ridiculous, yet MLMs persist. A seemingly endless supply of sellers are waiting to join these schemes, and the MLM industry is growing. But extensive research by Jon Taylor, president of the Consumer Awareness Institute, concludes that as many as 99 percent of those who do join make no money or even *lose* money. It boggles the mind that this is even an industry, let alone a thriving one with a large lobby in Washington, but there are reasons upon reasons upon reasons why, for it is *by design.* And the designers are more powerful and nefarious than you'd ever imagine.

When you say this directly to the faces of network marketers, or MLMers, as I have hundreds of times now, they usually come back with some version of the following:

All businesses are networks.
All stores have groups of customers.
All successful products have a following.

Direct sales, they say, is exactly the same as having your own store on Main Street, except you don't have to work Main Street hours and there's no boss and you don't have to pay rent. When you counter with a million *Yeah, but*s, including "But that store on Main Street doesn't *have to* franchise to stay in business," that's when you get to tell them about franchise law and how MLMs avoid following it.

Another phrase defenders love to throw out is "MLMs aren't pyramid schemes because pyramid schemes are illegal." That's like saying someone is not a murderer because the person hasn't been caught yet. The evidence needed for the FTC to file suit against an MLM is the hardest evidence to gather because an overwhelming number of participants must admit to being suckered and suckering others.

In these pages you will learn how the industry preys upon the financially precarious, such as stay-at-home moms or undocumented or disabled workers; how the money at the top of more than one MLM can secure political power; how the shame and financial stress of being involved in an MLM can cost people their life savings and bankrupt their dreams even when it leaves them some savings. We'll answer why it is so hard for us to see a scam for what it is, what about our brains keeps us from admitting defeat, and why, in the face of all evidence to the contrary, the dominant narrative of MLMs is one of abundance and freedom from financial stress.

Knowing the truth about MLMs and how much money, time, and trust people put into them while the folks in charge sit counting their gold Scrooge McDuck–style is a hard truth to live with, trust me. But I have hope. Silence and secrecy have kept these companies in business, and they're about to be exposed, scrutinized in ways they've been running from (and litigating out of) for decades.

From the very beginning of this business model, which grew rapidly in the early twentieth century, powerful characters have shaped the way MLMs do business. We'll look at what kinds of people *invented* this system where almost everyone who is promised money actually loses it. Through their own words, we'll get to know the founders of Tupperware, Amway, and others.

These schemes have spent untold millions lobbying for the industry, even after the FTC began taking some companies down by proving they are pyramid schemes. But those takedowns only resulted in a bolstering of the rights of MLMs and their owners. It's a truly American story that the bad actors continue to fail up.

Why do we keep falling for it? What in our nature, or our sense of American exceptionalism, or our idea that this place is a meritocracy where grit and determination equate to wealth, keeps us in their clutches? Is something inherently wrong with us, or are we at the mercy of forces so large and powerful that, short of a political revolution, we will never overcome?

Most important perhaps, we'll look at the stories of those at the very bottom. Those of us who have wanted desperately for the promises to come true. To be our own boss, to work our own hours, to spend time with our families, all while earning whatever amount of money we write in our manifestation journal every morning. Who are we, the churning millions who go into MLMs, fail, and are quickly replaced by the hordes of bright, eager, and optimistic workers who wishfully believe there is a better, easier way to earn a living?

1

Anatomy
of a Scheme

When I spoke to Julie in 2022, it had been twelve years since she married her first husband. While they were still newlyweds, Mira, the wife of one of his friends, invited Julie to a girls' night. The invitation came with the promise of snacks, drinks, new pals, and an opportunity to buy dildos at a discount from a company called Pure Romance. Julie accepted the invitation enthusiastically. She was brand new to the east coast and was just getting to know the women in her husband's circle. He'd been in the military for a few years before Julie met him and had a whole community of friends, and she wanted to ingratiate herself with them. Plus, she had a feeling it would be fun.

Without asking, Julie had assumed this was probably a multi-level-marketing affair, a concept she was familiar with, having grown up around Avon ladies and Tupperware parties. So, on the evening of the gathering, she filled a jug with homemade sweet tea and headed to Mira's place, a ranch-style suburban home set among dozens of look-alikes about fifteen minutes from where Julie lived. She entered through the door off the kitchen—as you do in the suburbs for some reason even though everyone has a nice front door—and made her way to the living room, where she was greeted by Mira and nine other women she'd never met, all of whom seemed to already know one another. At just twenty-three, fresh out of college and starting out in a new adult life in this new community, she noticed she was one of the youngest people there; guessing (because who would go to a stranger's house and start asking people how old they were?), she thought most of the women were in their thirties, with a few a generation older than that. It was immediately not the kind of fun she'd been expecting. She felt awkward, but it was too late to turn back.

Moments after Julie walked in, one of the women handed her a small catalog. She looked to be a few years older than Julie, but, to hear Julie tell it, way cooler. She was blond for one, tattooed for two, and "kinda funky." She introduced herself as Shawna and invited Julie to find a seat and relax. So Julie sat down and started thumbing through the catalog of "bedroom accessories," which included lingerie, massage oils, and sex toys.

Despite growing up in the Bible Belt and receiving an abstinence-only education, the thought of being sold sex toys in a roomful of strangers didn't bother Julie. "I'm very progressive with a lot of my views on things, so I was open to it," she says. "I've been in . . . an adult toy shop before where it was this creepy guy working behind the counter, so I liked the idea of having a woman to talk with me and to answer my questions and things like that." Her only wish was that this wasn't the *first* time meeting most of the women.

"Before we get too far, I'm gonna tell you about myself so you feel more comfortable with me, and then we're gonna play a game," Shawna began. She said she was a wife, and a mother to one little boy, and that this party business was her husband's idea. Men weren't allowed to sell for Pure Romance, but he liked the products and had encouraged Shawna to get involved. She told the room she had signed up as a consultant about three months prior, speaking about the experience as if it was a fun hobby, an excuse to socialize. "I get to go out, I just have fun and get away from, you know, my husband and my toddler for the night," Shawna said. "I get to have girls' nights every weekend," the ominous implication being that her social life would have been nonexistent were it not disguised as work.

As guests thumbed through catalogs, Shawna began passing around products, first bath supplies and lotions, then sex toys such as bullet vibrators and dildos. While most of the women seemed fine handling and examining the various items, Julie noticed that the woman seated directly to her right picked each one up between her thumb and forefinger as if it were a used condom and quickly tossed it to the next person. Her prudishness made everyone giggle.

Then Shawna introduced a game that was kind of like an adult Mad Libs: "Pick your favorite celebrity, male or female. You're going on a vacation together. Then choose an action, whether it's hug, kiss, touch, caress, massage, whatever. And then pick two body parts." This was meant to be an icebreaker, and it worked. "So people were saying things like 'Hi, my name is Candy, and I am going to go to Jamaica with Emma Watson, and I am going to touch her arm with my boob,' and people got so funny," Julie recalls. "Someone said, 'I'm gonna touch their eyeball with my nipple,' and that got people laughing *and* thinking about touch." She said this was more silly than embarrassing, but still awkward seeing as how she was kind of the odd woman out and hadn't talked to most of these women about anything else thus far. But Julie warmed up quickly to this new crowd, and they liked how young and inexperienced she seemed.

Nothing like a newlywed in the room to make a sex-toy party even more hilarious.

Shawna then announced a raffle. These party-based MLMs are chockablock full of games and gimmicks, prizes and applause. That's by design: without the fanfare, you're clearly just getting a sales pitch, and MLMs thrive on making their business model not look like work. So, these companies come up with ways to keep the audience engaged. In Shawna's raffle, for every question a guest asked, the guest got a raffle ticket to win some products Shawna had brought with her, mostly the low-price bath products. "Feel free to ask all about my business, just not my"—here she ran her fingers up and down her body—"*business*," Shawna joked. Arms shot up and people began spewing out anything they could think of in a frantic raffle-ticket grab. When Shawna announced the winners, they squealed in delight or jealousy as they were handed little bottles of bath gel or lube. When the big contest ended, Shawna told the women they could come into the kitchen, one by one, and discreetly place their orders with her. Julie jumped to her feet. She thought this might be the perfect way to widen her nonexistent social circle—by inviting herself into her neighbors' homes to have a silly time. Julie ran to the kitchen and picked out some shaving cream and a set of microwavable silicone hearts meant to be used like hot stones for a massage, knowing her husband would love the surprise. But the products weren't what made her race to the front of the line. Julie wanted to know more about Shawna's job and how to get involved.

Julie was working full-time as a social worker and going to culinary school to become a pastry chef, but the idea of selling sex toys on the side and pocketing some extra cash sounded easy and super fun and like a great way to meet people. She was also excited by how sex positive the company and the experience seemed, and she liked the idea of being able to teach other women about their sexuality and erase some of the shame and stigma that so often comes with talking about your sex life. "I grew up with that whole 'If you have sex, you're gonna get a disease and die,' so I was interested in the whole thing."

To get started, Shawna explained, all you had to do was purchase one of four Pure Romance starter kits, which consisted of catalogs, some order forms, a training booklet, and products to use for demonstration and sale. Julie went for one of the less expensive options, a $99 kit that included some of the company's most basic products. "It might've been ten products total," Julie recalls. "A few bath items, a body spray, and two or three bedroom accessories."

She was told there were two ways to make money working for Pure Romance. She was *not* told that the pay structure would be so convoluted and difficult to understand that she never knew *what* she was making until the checks came in. The first way to make money was by selling products directly to customers at parties or on the street or, heck, to yourself or your mom. This was paid by commission, a certain percentage of the retail price. I understand it to be sort of a discount or rebate, ultimately. A sort of perpetual sale price depending on the level you're at in the company.

The second way to make money was by recruiting other women—remember, no men allowed!—to sell products for the organization. Shawna explained that when you recruited someone, you immediately made a commission when the woman bought a starter kit, which the company counted as a "sale," *and* you got a bonus for signing the person up. Recruits also made you money once you had enough of them in your "downline," which was pitched as a sort of team of employees. The bigger your downline, the higher your rank in the company, and the larger your commission percentage. The ultimate goal was for your downline to create their own downlines; that's where the real money was. Here's an illustration of how that was supposed to work:

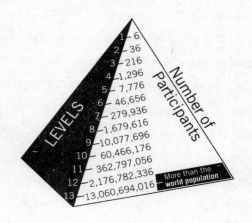

Julie was Shawna's first-ever recruit. And a month later, Shawna quit. But that didn't bother Julie. "I knew that people went in and out of these companies all the time. I knew that there was like some high turnover that sometimes you talked to somebody and they weren't doing it anymore, even though you just had a party with them like a month before, so it didn't raise any flags to me or anything." When an upline quits, it's rare that someone in the person's downline gets promoted, so this was a neutral event for Julie. Usually, the quitter's downline gets absorbed by someone with the same rank in a lateral move, so Julie was just absorbed into another rep's downline.

At the time Julie joined, Pure Romance sold about one hundred different products, but she says her starter pack only came with some "bottom-of-the-line" stuff. She wanted to get her hands on some of the bestsellers, higher-ticket items that the women at the party seemed to have gone gaga over—cock rings, or *C rings* in Pure Romance parlance, and wireless vibrators in particular. That meant she had to shell out more cash up front to get her business started in a way that she was told would ultimately make her more successful. She dipped into savings and right away spent $150 for extra demo items. Over the next six months Julie estimates she spent about $1,000 just sprucing up her kit. That's $1,000 that her upline would make a commission on as a sale, mind you.

Before she could start throwing her own parties, Julie also had to take a few hours of sex ed training so she could properly explain and demonstrate how everything was supposed to *work*. She took courses on human anatomy and female sexuality, which she found genuinely educational and interesting, if limited, since they focused almost exclusively on heterosexual sex. She was also required to attend a few parties run by more senior distributors to observe and take notes on how the big dogs operated, what tactics they used to recruit others, and how they demonstrated the products. She invested a lot of time up front before she saw a dollar, but it seemed worth it because at these events Julie first heard about the potential to get very, very rich.

"They explained that to start we'd take home thirty-five percent of what we sold," she recalls. " 'If you want this to be a hobby, you're only going to make one hundred or two hundred dollars a month. If you want this to be your part-time job, your commission will go up based on sales, and you can make five hundred to a thousand dollars. And then, if you want this to be your full-time job, earnings are *unlimited*.' " So, let's just pause and get that straight. You could make $100 *or* bajillions of dollars. It all depended on whether you *wanted* to or not. *Interesting*.

Julie also learned that eager recruits could leapfrog a few levels, raking in a 40 to 50 percent commission right out of the gate by purchasing a much more expensive starter pack. The first level in Pure Romance at the time was *consultant*, then you could earn 40 percent commissions when you reached the next rank, *advanced consultant*; 50 percent commissions kicked in at *senior consultant*. (The five levels above that all had different versions of the title *director*.) Taking home that much sounded wonderful to Julie, but she couldn't afford a big lump sum right at the beginning, so she would have to rise through the ranks the hard way: by recruiting her own team and meeting quarterly sales goals. One hidden factoid that came to light during these trainings was that minimum retail sales benchmarks were tied to your title and commission level. If you didn't reach those minimums every month or quarter, you'd be bumped back down the ladder. The stakes were high to somehow keep the cash flowing upward, month after month.

After Julie finished all the hours of required-yet-unpaid training, she hosted her first party. All she needed was a host and a guest list. Her mother volunteered to host the event at her home, noting that it was nicer than Julie's and would make a better first impression. "And then she invited her friends," Julie says. Those friends included Julie's sister and aunt.

"Mind you, I had been taught all of these sales pitches that the top earners use. These are the girls that are being picked to be corporate trainers, that corporate is flying across the U.S., the women that are chummy-chummy with the founders of the company. So I'm like, 'I'm going to say what they're saying.' So here I am in front of everyone trying to sell a male masturbation sleeve. I demoed it the way I was taught: I have the sleeve in my hand and I'm using another toy, sliding it up and down. And I tell them you're supposed to blindfold your partner, utilize the sleeve on them, then put a little bit of lubrication on your mouth to make it look like you have done something! I did *all* of this. At my first party. With my mother."

Julie sold $700 in products that night, which meant with her 35 percent commission she earned $245, but she got zero recruits. Putting together her initial sign-up fee and the extra $150 she spent on the demonstration items, it would seem that Julie just about broke even, which in any business is a great start. Julie was hopeful. It took her many months, but eventually she had "six or seven" women in her downline at any time. People came and went at a quick pace, but each of those women had to buy starter kits, so Julie earned a good commission there even if her team wasn't growing as fast as she'd have liked. And she was continuing to hold parties, selling at least as much in retail as she did that first night.

"I thought I was making good money," Julie says. "I thought I was making about like eleven hundred dollars a month. But I wasn't taking into account any expenses. When you do your training, you go over every page and they don't speak on any of that. There is no training on accounting. There is no information on recording your expenses. Not once. Nobody talks to you about logging hours. You know, how much time has been spent on your cell phone. I was not factoring in the fact that I had to start buying catalogs and order forms. I wasn't taking into account that I had purchased some inventory; that I was constantly driving to seven different cities to throw parties." Julie was riding high on the $1,000 checks she was receiving, a sure sign that she was doing something right and making her way to the pot of gold at the end of the double-ended dildo.

It took a few years, but she eventually recruited her way up to director status, which paid a 50 percent commission. But that also required Julie to personally sell $1,000 in retail items and for her team to turn over $2,000 every month. So that's $3,000 a month in sex toys in and around coastal Virginia. To achieve that, and to keep new recruits on deck, Julie started throwing parties every single weekend, hustling to make both her personal sales goals and those of her downline. You can't just tell your downlines that the key to success is partying, you have to walk the walk and hope they follow suit with their own packed party schedules. To hit the team quotas, she'd also spend a lot of time recruiting. The initial sign-up fees counted toward these sales goals, so if there weren't a lot of retail sales being made to strangers at parties, no worries. Just recruit someone new and you'd be able to keep your numbers up.

At first, it was fun and easy. Novelty went a long way in the early days with people at least being curious enough about the pitch to agree to host a party. But a paradoxical thing started to happen the more she excelled at recruiting. As time went on and more people in her area joined Pure Romance, there were fewer people to make those initial sign-up sales to. Everyone who wanted to sign up with Pure Romance had, and she ran out of customers outside of the company. Julie realized she had to go farther afield to find eager customers and spend more and more of her time planning parties in neighboring communities. Then she found out the sex toys Pure Romance sold were made by a giant manufacturer called California Exotics, which was supplying pretty much every other mainstream outlet, including the popular adult chain Adam & Eve and Amazon, with the exact same products. The retail prices elsewhere were about a third of Pure Romance's, Julie estimates. This was shocking, but she kept her eye on the millions.

She surmised the value in her business was the social aspect, the parties and friendship, so she pushed it as hard as she could, recruiting friends and colleagues, strangers on the street, a woman who worked at the same doctor's office as Julie's sister. Finally, she recruited a friend of a friend who had no car, no money, and no real knack for shilling bedroom accessories. Julie had started to feel desperate, and her pocketbook reflected that. Here she was still going to culinary school, still working her day job, and now she had this side hustle that was supposed to make her millions but was actually adding work and stress but not much in extra income. How could this be? Answers, she was assured, would be found at the annual Pure Romance convention, which she, as a director, was required to attend. At her own expense, of course.

That weekend, Julie and three other director-level reps from her area piled into one car and drove nine hours to Cincinnati, where Pure Romance is based. They each had to pay a $400 registration fee, which notably didn't include the cost of food, travel, or the one-night hotel stay. Once at the conference, Julie went to a few of the business-oriented seminars, but they were just repeating the same basic information she had learned at the beginning, and that she would give to her own recruits. Nowhere were there any answers as to how she was supposed to achieve the multimillion-dollar dream that had been promised to her. It was not the miracle she'd been hoping for.

That night, the four women bunked in one room with two double beds. Even though they were very busy, the women were cash-poor, sinking more money into the scheme than they were taking out. Had they had enough money to get their own rooms, they wouldn't need the help they were promised at the conference. Julie only kind-of knew one of the women prior to this trip; the rest were strangers, other area reps with whom, at best, she may have exchanged an email or two. Before bed that night, the women talked about why they were involved with the company and what had brought them to the conference. Julie's bedmate, whom she'd just met when the woman picked Julie up earlier that day, told her she was selling Pure Romance to cover IVF bills. She was living paycheck to paycheck at her other job and saw hope in this enterprise. Julie's heart broke for her, but a light bulb also went off.

"She was concerned at one point if her vehicle was even gonna make it," Julie recalls. "I sat down and I started talking to her and realized that I needed to start monitoring where all the money was going, because I just couldn't fathom it. How are you working a full-time job and you're doing your Pure Romance *and* you are living paycheck to paycheck?"

Then Julie realized she had the same question about her own experience in Pure Romance. If she really thought about it, she didn't have much to show for all the time and effort she was putting into her business. The day she got back from the conference, Julie nervously sat down and did something she'd avoided since she first signed up: she crunched some numbers. What she found at the end of a day spent plugging away at spreadsheets shocked her: after four years of selling and seeking out new training, she was *still* taking home roughly $1,000 a month in commissions, which was the bare minimum she needed to keep her title and the 50 percent commission she'd worked so hard to earn. "When I actually started to do the math, I was making less than minimum wage." In fact, Julie says, she was barely breaking even.

One of the big expenses Julie still hadn't accounted for was her increasing inventory. MLMs are not supposed to encourage their sellers to stock inventory, but Julie says her upline definitely did, reminding her that if she had items on hand to sell at parties, they would move quicker than if she had to order them and make customers wait. She estimates that, toward the end, she always had around $4,000 worth of product in her trunk, often using her party commissions to replenish her supply.

The final straw came a few months before she ultimately quit Pure Romance: she found herself coming up short, not selling near the $3,000 in goods required of her and her team. She decided that rather than lose her status in the company, she'd just buy the balance using her credit card. As soon as she did it, a wave of regret and shame washed over her. Suddenly, the scales fell from her eyes. "It was like a water slide where you start really high and find yourself in the deep end." She quit, and to this day, she's still afraid to look at her numbers too closely. Julie can only guess that she lost around $10,000 in all during her time with Pure Romance.

Julie's story is normal in the world of multi-level marketing. According to the Direct Selling Association, or the DSA, which is the main lobbying group for the MLM industry, 7.3 million people were registered sellers with an MLM in the United States in 2021.[1] The DSA and its more than five hundred member companies tout their industry as an extraordinary business opportunity for those millions of people. The recruiting page of one distributor's Pure Romance website[2] presents a pitch pretty similar to the one Julie heard on that couch back in 2011. "We're not gonna lie—it pays to have fun (literally). Side gig or full-time, it's up to you! Use your Pure Romance profits to pay off debt, save for the family vacation, put money towards retirement . . . whatever you need. Whether you want to sell directly to friends, work from home and share your business online, or get the in-home party started, hustling hard yields big results."

"Hard work equals more money" is always the refrain. Yet in reality, 99 percent of people who participate in MLMs *lose* money.[3] That means that of the 7,300,000 people currently involved in an MLM, 7,227,000 will end up in the hole— just like Julie. As I said, it's normal. The internet is chockablock full of stories from former MLMers who lost their life savings—and typically a few friends along the way—after sinking money into their "businesses" thinking that if they just recruited *one* more person or ascended *one* more level in the company, they could make it big. Sure, out of the thousands of people who do earn money, you can find some winners, but those who come out with even $1 are counted in the 1 percent.

These statistics are not hard to come by. Mainstream media outlets have been covering MLMs for years, and a popular 2016 documentary, *Betting on Zero*, followed billionaire hedge-fund investor Bill Ackman's mission to expose the MLM giant Herbalife, which sells nutritional supplements and diet shakes, as a pyramid scheme. John Oliver's hilariously biting segment on MLMs, released the same year, has garnered over 30 million views on his show *Last Week Tonight*'s YouTube channel. *LuLaRich,* a 2021 four-part doc from Amazon about the downfall of the knitwear MLM LuLaRoe, was released to rave reviews. Discovery+ soon followed up with their own documentary on the company, *The Rise and Fall of LuLaRoe.*

Meanwhile, hashtags, profiles, and discussion boards dedicated to exposing the financial realities of these companies are all over social media. The anti-MLM subreddit has nearly a million members and climbing. The YouTube channel The Recovering Hunbot (named after the pejorative term *hun* often used to describe MLMers, who are known to start out texts or emails to potential recruits with "Hey hun!" regardless of how close they are with the person) has gained hundreds of thousands of views with videos delving into the dubious business practices of today's top MLMs. On a podcast called *Sounds like MLM but OK,* the hosts regularly pick apart the actions of these same huns.

The federal government has, for decades, been investigating various MLMs under suspicion they could be illegal pyramid schemes. In an extremely high-profile case, the Federal Trade Commission (the government body responsible for protecting consumers from fraud, dishonest advertising, and dangerous products) sued Herbalife in 2014, alleging that the company's compensation program "incentivizes not retail sales, but the recruiting of additional participants who will fuel the enterprise by making wholesale purchases of product," and that therefore "the overwhelming majority of Herbalife Distributors who pursue the business opportunity make little or no money, and a substantial percentage lose money."[4] The company, worth over $3 billion, settled the suit for $200 million in 2016 and agreed to change its business model so that sellers no longer earned money on recruitment. In exchange, Herbalife was allowed to continue operation, and the chairwoman of the FTC declared, comically, that the company was "not determined not to have been a pyramid" scheme.[5]

This distinction—whether MLMs are pyramid schemes or not—is a matter of intense debate among those who follow the industry. The FTC has on its website a handy and brief guide to that distinction:

There are two tell-tale signs that a product is simply being used to disguise a pyramid scheme: inventory loading and a lack of retail sales. Inventory loading occurs when a company's incentive program forces recruits to buy more products than they could ever sell, often at inflated prices. If this occurs throughout the company's distribution system, the people at the top of the pyramid reap substantial profits, even though little or no product moves to market. The people at the bottom make excessive payments for inventory that simply accumulates in their basements.

A lack of retail sales is also a red flag that a pyramid exists. Many pyramid schemes will claim that their product is selling like hot cakes. However, on closer examination, the sales occur only between people inside the pyramid structure or to new recruits joining the structure, not to consumers out in the general public.[6]

Critics of MLMs argue that these companies meet the definition of an illegal pyramid scheme because the vast majority of purchases are being made by people within the company, sometimes by people like Julie purchasing extra product to meet sales goals for the month or to load a trunk with product. But foremost, sales are being made to new recruits who are buying in for selling by themselves.

Defenders, on the other hand, say no, anyone *using the product* is a retail customer, whether signed up to sell or not. The DSA even made up a new category of sales rep called a *preferred buyer*, which is a person who signs up to get the discount but doesn't try to build a downline. Pretty tricky, right? Ultimately, none of these companies is incentivized to keep track of who those people are, whether they change their mind and try recruiting the next day or week or month, and who actually uses the products once they leave the warehouse.

Here's another issue: in traditional retail businesses the re-tailer purchases products at a discount from the wholesaler or manufacturer, sells it to consumers at a markup, and pockets the difference. If something doesn't fly off the shelves, the re-tailers are not obligated to buy it again. They can also put items that aren't selling on clearance or place two competing products right next to each other to entice Coca-Cola fans to try a cola that's ten cents cheaper. MLMs, in contrast, tend to have extremely specific rules about how their products can be sold—the prices are often fixed, which means you can't mark down old or less desirable products or offer promotions to encourage people to buy more. You can't sell competing products at the same time. And many of these companies have incredibly narrow refund policies, exempting seasonal or "special" items, giving tight turnaround times for returns, or discontinuing a product, therefore making it not "resalable." This is how people end up with thousands of LuLaRoe leg-gings gathering dust in their garage.

And we haven't even talked about whether the products are worth the retail price *or* the discounted price. MLM products are usually fairly expensive and not that different from similar products you can find in a retail store. At the time of this writ-ing, for example, Pure Romance offers seven types of rabbit vibrators, six of which retail for more than $100. Meanwhile, the popular sex-toy site Adam & Eve—which Julie confirmed sells the *exact same line of sex toys* as Pure Romance—offers seventy-two varieties of the same type of vibrator, two-thirds of which retail for *less* than $100.[7] A bottle of Pure Romance's Hybrid Gel Lubricant sells for $18 per 1.7-ounce bottle.[8] A bottle of the old stalwart K-Y Jelly twice the size? Less than $7 on Amazon.[9]

When you start to examine how this all works, it starts to look an awful lot like a pyramid scheme. Yet, even when the government investigates MLMs, it almost always stops short of categorizing them as pyramid schemes. There are big, institutional, creepy reasons for that, which we'll get to. Meanwhile, unsuspecting people hoping to make a better life for themselves sign up to join MLMs every day.

According to the DSA, in the decade leading up to 2019, MLM sales grew from $29.6 billion to $35.2 billion. Even though this is a fraction of the nearly $5.5 trillion in overall retail sales in the United States for the same period, it still points to remarkable growth.

As I'm writing this in the summer of 2022, MLMs have just experienced something of an industry boom. In 2020, as the economy shut down and millions of people lost their jobs, the MLM industry had one of its best years in recent memory. Sensing an opportunity to appeal to the newly unemployed, as well as those who wanted to work from home and/or needed additional flexibility in their schedules to take care of their children but couldn't afford to *not* work, many MLM companies ramped up recruitment, offering an alternative to traditional jobs. And it worked. In 2020 alone, the number of direct sellers working for MLMs rose by 13.2 percent, and despite a dip in retail sales across the board, direct sales increased by 13.9 percent.[10] The retail sales went up just as much as the participation in MLMs? So, in 2020 the number of people selling MLM products increased almost exactly as much as the sales increased? I'm no mathematician, but it seems clear the dragon is eating its own tail.

It wasn't just the job opportunity that appealed to people during this time. MLMs are also a bastion of wellness products such as vitamins, supplements, dietary shakes, nutrition bars, and even essential oils, many of which claim to help boost immunity or ward off viruses. COVID-19 presented quite the marketing opportunity, and many of these brands preyed on public fears around the virus. Arbonne, a maker of protein shakes and makeup, pivoted to COVID prevention in 2020, with many sellers claiming a product called Immunity Support could prevent an infection.

The people at the top of these companies, the fraction of the 1 percent who make any money to speak of, know all of this and continue to sing the business model's praises while blaming the bottom rung for not working hard enough to reach the top. This "industry" has so many obvious flaws that it's surprising not much is being done to stop it. Every MLM is a little bit different, which makes the industry hard to go after as a whole. Some companies are selling banana-print leggings with holes in them, but some are selling bags that function as bags and are purchased by people who want bags. Some are more egregious in their financial promises than others. Some have been around for decades, some for just a couple of months. Only a dozen or so are publicly traded, so it's hard to get data on how well anyone is doing, or how poorly, and also because the sellers are "independent retailers" and not employees. This isn't a problem for the companies, though. It makes it easy for them to claim that all of their sales are to people outside the organization because no one is keeping track of where anything ends up. The only money coming in might be from new recruits buying starter packs, but because the heads of these companies don't ask where their goods are going, they can claim plausible deniability when asked whether there are any outside sales at all, to real customers who are not recruits. The companies do put a lot of rules in writing about what you can and can't say about a product, that you can't make false promises about what it does or how rich it'll make someone, but the industry relies on the companies to regulate all of that themselves. There is absolutely no oversight or enforcement of whether participants are following the "rules"; most often they're going to follow the direction of their uplines, as Julie did. Unlike in other self-regulating industries such as health care or education, no one has a license to be revoked, and the companies can feign ignorance and blame any misdeed the FTC catches on some rogue agent on the bottom rung.

There's also a big difference between ethics and legality, and MLMs seem less interested in whether they *should* be roping financially desperate people into their schemes and leading them into debt than whether the FTC *can* slap them with a lawsuit. Not many industries would brag about how anyone, with zero experience in any type of job, can spend their last few hundred dollars to join a company that offers no benefits, no cost-of-living wage, and no way to recoup losses, and that by doing so they have a 1 percent chance of earning more than one cent. If you worked at your local CVS and no one shopped there, or if you worked on commission for a pharmaceutical company but no one bought your product, you would eventually lose your job, but you wouldn't end up in debt to the company.

Pretend for a moment that what companies are promising is *actually* possible. That through sheer determination, one has the opportunity to strike it rich. That this society we've built is a meritocracy and all you need is grit and charm to reap its rewards. Despite all evidence to the contrary—the pay gap, the prison industrial complex, record corporate profits, and the concentration of wealth—we are, to a person, raised to believe that all you need is to want success badly enough. We've all bought into this fantasy, and we're all paying the price.

So, why isn't anyone doing anything? Don't throw your hands up just yet, because we're going on a ride to find out how we keep getting fooled, why we find it so hard to get out once we're in, and why the dominant narrative around MLMs isn't one of woe but one of enviable success. Exploring the origins of these schemes and their key architects is a fascinating journey into the human psyche—into mass delusion and hysteria, illogical decision-making, and grandiose visions; larger-than-life con artists; and politicians who are bought and paid to look the other way. It's a journey into the current state of the American Dream.

2

Women's Work

It's a stretch to say I wouldn't be here without Avon, but I wouldn't be *here*, writing this book, without Avon. I cannot remember a time in my life when I didn't know about Avon. My great-grandmother Maxine became an Avon lady before I was even born, so some of my earliest sense memories of growing up in the 1980s are the smells of the lipstick samples she used to bring home and let us kids play with. You know how most little kids play grocery store or restaurant or doctor? My aunt Amy and I would take turns playing Avon lady, applying lipstick and blush to each other from Grandma Max's samples. Amy was six years older than me so obviously a much better Avon lady. We could use Grandma's old order forms and catalogs and a disconnected rotary phone to "call" around and check on our sales force and customers. Was everyone getting what she needed? Any new orders that day? Any difficulties selling anything?

Grandma Maxine got into Avon later in life, shortly after the death of her husband, my great-grandfather Leo. Maxine was born relatively well-off in rural Michigan, her dad being a veterinarian. Family lore has it she wore fur coats to school and was a well-trained pianist, the latter of which I know to be true because she was my teacher when I was a kid. She had incredible nails, long and slender, perfectly groomed and painted. A real Betty Draper kind of situation. But her dad ran off when she was six years old, leaving the family destitute. When she was fourteen, she met and married my great-grandfather. Maxine languished in that relationship, poor as dirt with four kids to feed, until her husband kicked the bucket. That's when Avon came calling, bringing with it a sense of independence and glamour that she'd been missing for decades. She never made real money with the company so far as anyone can tell, but the purpose and self-esteem and companionship she found there definitely kept her spirit alive. After all, in our society much of our worth is measured in dollars, and if she could sell even one lipstick to another person, that was positive reinforcement that she was playing the game right.

Just as I wouldn't be here without Avon, Avon—and

pretty much every multi-level-marketing company that's ever existed—would not be here without women like my grandma Maxine. Women make up 74 percent[1] of the MLM workforce, and the overwhelming majority of MLM companies sell things that are traditionally known as women's products. Avon sells makeup. So do Mary Kay, LimeLife, Arbonne, Younique, Beautycounter, and countless others. LuLaRoe sells cutesy printed leggings, dresses, and other comfortable clothes made out of stretchy fabrics that are specifically marketed to, and subsequently popular with, moms all over the country. It Works! sells body-sculpting products, such as "fat-melting" stomach wraps. dōTERRA and Young Living sell scented essential oils. Even MLMs that are more gender-neutral in their branding—think Herbalife, Amway, Beachbody—sell products (nutritional supplements, household cleansers and personal-care products, and fitness classes, respectively) that are thought to appeal to women.

Why are women such a presence in this world of network marketing? Why are they targeted to be both its most prominent sellers and its most prolific buyers? Simple: in the United States, women control—either by actually swiping the credit card or by convincing someone else in the family to do so—80 percent of household financial decisions.[2] This goes for everything from small-ticket items such as groceries and clothing, to larger decisions such as car purchases, all the way up to the house that will become said household. And women still (sigh) do the majority of the child-rearing and house-keeping.[3] This means that the promises MLMs make are particularly appealing to women, especially those with children: you can earn money on a flexible schedule that allows you to do all the unpaid labor you're strapped with.

In many ways, the MLM model was built—sometimes purposefully, sometimes purely by circumstance—with women at its center. Thanks to the work of a few pioneering individuals, modern-day MLMs have a long tradition of women-centric recruitment and sales strategies to build upon.

Avon Calling

The story of how MLMs became women's work starts with the history of door-to-door sales. Traveling salesmen have been peddling all kinds of things to all kinds of folks since the beginning of civilization. I sell rice, you don't have any rice nearby, I show up with rice once in a while, and we trade. That's all trade was for a very, very long time, just dudes wandering around like, "Chickens! Get your chickens here!" Whether called a *peddler* or *huckster* or even *costermonger* (for real!), they were all doing the same thing: wandering around and sometimes knocking on actual doors to sell products. They always had a likability problem due to their perpetual outsider status. The scribe Ben Sira even negs these dudes in

Ecclesiasticus 26:29: "A merchant shall hardly keep himself from doing wrong; and an huckster shall not be freed from sin."[4] Relax, Ben!

We have plenty of evidence from about four thousand years ago of a trade route between what are now Iraq and Turkey. Men would leave their wives behind for years to make this trek, bringing along donkeys loaded up with all kinds of junk. Wild animals were everywhere and hungry, and all along the trail the beer was flowing. You can picture the scene. These men were *rough*. Nothing like the buttoned-up Willy Loman door-to-door salesman archetype we reference today, which only came along in the twentieth century. No, before that, these guys were gnarly.

When Europeans came to the Americas, it was more of the same among them until around the time of the Industrial Revolution, in the latter half of the nineteenth century. Technological advances in manufacturing—of textiles, ironworks, machinery—meant that new products were popping up more rapidly than ever before, and novelty is a great driver of sales. Imagine you're a housewife out on the prairie who has been doing laundry using a bucket and a washboard and suddenly a strange man shows up to sell you a hand-crank washing machine. Maybe you don't *need* one, but if you have a few bucks lying around, boy, it sure would be nice. So there's a boom in new products to sell and better ways of getting around the country (trains!) to sell them, and thus door-to-door selling really took off. It wasn't all novelty of course. These peddlers hawked basic wares such as cloth, soap, and whiskey in the rural areas, where most Americans lived. They played a necessary part in American expansion westward.

One of the most famous of these men was Levi Strauss. Levi, born in Bavaria in 1829, moved to New York in 1848 to work for his older brothers' wholesale dry-goods business. When the Gold Rush came about, he headed to California to expand the family business and traveled up and down the West Coast selling soap and socks and all manner of boring things you need to sustain life as a prospector, including pants. In 1872, Levi got a letter from one of his clients in Nevada, a tailor named Jacob Davis. Davis had figured out a way to use rivets to reinforce pockets and seams on denim pants and asked Strauss to partner with him to manufacture them. Here was a product that had it all: a novel breakthrough in a daily staple. And the rest is history.

Levi was far from alone in his frontier-spiritedness. This was a time of massive immigration. In 1850, only 2 million people in the United States were foreign-born. By 1880, just thirty years later, that number had bloomed to close to 7 million. What were these millions meant to do right off the boat if they didn't have jobs waiting for them? One option was knocking on the doors of others who'd fled the same lands they had.

A standout among door-to-door salesmen of the era was

David McConnell, founder of Avon, which would become one of the longest-running and highest-volume MLMs in history. McConnell is our first character in the Avon story. He was a door-to-door book salesman. He didn't like it, but he was good at it, so he got promoted and started training a bunch of other salespeople all over the eastern United States. He was so good that in 1886 he bought Union Publishing Company, the publishing house he'd been working for. There are several theories as to how he turned a book publisher into a beauty business: some say he started handing out perfume samples as a bribe to get housewives to listen to him pitch them a set of encyclopedias, while others claim he wanted to find something his female sales associates could sell because they were lousy at selling books. "We had a number of lady travelers that were not as successful . . . so I wanted to get hold of something that they could handle to the trade, and I lighted on a box of Perfumery," McConnell claimed in one of his many writings on the history of Avon—done through letters, bulletins to salespeople, and eventually a brief autobiography.

In that "official" recounting, McConnell offers a third, less folkloric version of the origin story: "My ambition was to manufacture a line of goods that would be consumed, used up, and to sell it through canvassing agents, direct from the factory to the consumer. The starting of the perfume business was the result of most careful and thorough investigation. . . .

In investigating this matter nearly every line of business was gone over, and it seemed to me, then, as it has since been proven, that the perfume business in its different branches afforded the very best possible opportunity to build up a permanent and well-established trade."[5]

In 1892, he founded the California Perfume Company, so named because McConnell thought it sounded exotic and natural, even though the company was headquartered in New York.[6] It wasn't until 1939 that his son would change the name to Avon, an homage to Stratford-upon-Avon, where his father had once visited the home of William Shakespeare.

At first, McConnell stuck to perfume and manufactured his first five scents—violet, heliotrope, hyacinth, lily of the valley, and white rose—in "a space scarcely larger than an ordinary kitchen pantry."[7] Although McConnell claimed his homemade concoctions matched the quality of even the finest French colognes, the products he was selling were nothing special—and the company knew it. Decades later, in 1971, Avon's head of marketing, James E. Clitter, said as much in an interview with the *New York Times*: "We've never been great crusaders in new product ideas because the average housewife who is our representative is not about to explain them to her customer."[8] In other words, Avon's buyers and sellers weren't all that sophisticated, so the company could sell them any ole stuff and they won't know the difference.

While Avon wasn't breaking any ground with its products,

its main innovation was its decision to hire women to sell directly to other women. Remember the hordes of traveling salesmen that made up McConnell's competition? Among them were charlatans—snake-oil salesmen exploiting laypeople's ignorance about diseases and ailments. Homeless vagabonds who would skip town after selling off a batch of goods, never to be seen again. Women, McConnell correctly assumed, would trust other women—especially ones from their own community—far more than these fly-by-night characters, and he wanted to capitalize on that social currency.

According to company lore, the first Avon lady was Persis Foster Eames Albee, but friends called her PFE. Born in Maine, she got married sometime in her thirties to a man who became a state senator in New Hampshire. Meanwhile, Albee ran a little general store out of their house, which people just seemed to adore. Centrally located near the train station, with the town's only telephone, Albee's store was popular among both locals and visitors. In 1879, McConnell came through town and convinced her to stock some of his books in her store; they ended up flying off the shelves. McConnell was reported to be quite impressed with her talents. Things went along nicely that way for a few years until Albee's husband died in 1885, right around the time McConnell was futzing with the perfume idea. Aiming to sell a product for women that could be sold by women, McConnell immediately thought of Albee as a regional sales rep for the new product line. She said yes and became, essentially, the very first Avon Lady.[9] In old photographs, she looked and dressed just like the Dowager Countess from *Downton Abbey*. The year was 1886 and Albee was fifty years old.

The first beauty item the California Perfume Company (CPC) sold was the Little Dot Set, a collection of five perfumes in botanical scents. Given her status in the community, and that her store sold "holiday goods, household goods and ladies' furnishings" and housed that very hip telephone, Albee had easy entry to pretty much every home in town. As her success grew, back in New York, McConnell started adding more beauty products to the line—including soaps, lotions, and toothpaste. Soon, the story goes, area women Albee sold to began inquiring about becoming sales reps themselves. It sure beat working in fields or factories. McConnell made Albee a general agent for the Northeast and gave her his blessing to start building an army. A year into her tenure with the company Albee had recruited a dozen salespeople. She stuck around at CPC for twelve years,[10] eventually amassing what we'd now call a downline of five thousand women.[11]

Creating an all-female sales force had a number of obvious advantages for a direct-selling home-goods brand. For one thing, women are much less likely to kill or maim you when they come into your house. Think about it: you are a housewife, home alone, when a guy knocks on your door and asks if he can come in to show you this great new product he has to sell. You don't know this man. What if he's a thief or a murderer? And even if he's not, what will the neighbors think if they see you invite a random man into your house while your husband is at work? *And* he's trying to sell you perfume? Now, on the other hand, a friendly woman? Nothing improper or unsafe about that. And, heck, it could even be a nice distraction from housework and the kids.

To further combat the stereotype of the sleazy sales rep, McConnell and Albee also encouraged their crew to sell directly to people they already knew—friends, neighbors, relatives, fellow church congregants, and so forth.

This emphasis on trust and existing social networks came in particularly handy in the 1930s when several local governments around the country started passing legislation restricting the activities of door-to-door salesmen, after citizens began complaining that the salesmen were "irritating" and invading people's privacy (not unlike, say, how modern Americans complain about telemarketers and robocalls). In 1931, the Fuller Brush Company, which sold housewares door-to-door, sued the town of Green River, Wyoming, for creating an ordinance that prohibited door-to-door sales and lost. The Green River ordinance declared "peddlers, hawkers, itinerant merchants and transient vendors" a "nuisance" and declared door-to-door sales a misdemeanor. It is still used to this day as the basis upon which towns all over the United States prohibit people from banging on their residents' doors. It's worth noting that many of those "nuisances" were immigrants from Italy and Ireland and Jews from Eastern Europe, looking for economic opportunity in a new country.

In other words, these laws sprang from and were enforced through de facto racism. The California Perfume Company conveniently skirted this debate by going after another disenfranchised workforce: the homemaker. Femininity and motherliness assuaged fears more often than inspired them; solely employing sales*women*, McConnell thought, would allow his company to fly under the radar, because who would file a complaint about the nice lady up the street coming by for a visit to chat about perfume? CPC was thus unaffected by these laws and continued to sell its wares while steadily recruiting more and more people to do so.

Looking through early communications, such as sales brochures and bulletins, you can see how McConnell exploited certain aspects of femininity for his financial gain. He repeatedly spoke of unpleasant body odors that women could cover up with his perfumes and, as his offerings grew, encouraged women to purchase more of his goods for themselves. He compared those who didn't use CPC products to uncut diamonds. In one brochure, he claims, "The art of making women more attractive, more pleasing, has also taken the science and ingenuity of centuries." [12] Now, there existed an easy fix in his products.

But makeup wasn't the only thing CPC was selling. It was also selling *opportunity*, specifically the opportunity for women to earn money without having to take on traditional day jobs. Starting around 1905, the company began putting out marketing materials that promised new or would-be recruits "a business that is your very own." [13] This idea was extremely tempting, if a bit misleading. The women's suffrage movement was in full swing, and McConnell's pitch was highly appealing to independent thinkers. For those who were hesitant, McConnell emphasized that his sales force could work without sacrificing their responsibilities as wives and mothers. [14]

This recruiting strategy proved fruitful for CPC. By 1920, it had twenty thousand reps and had reached $1 million in annual sales. [15] Even after the Great Depression decimated the economy a decade later, the company continued to grow, thanks most likely to a huge cohort of women looking for alternative ways to earn money after they or their husbands lost their jobs. By the early 1960s, Avon employed more than 160,000 reps in the United States and had achieved $242 million in annual sales. [16]

Party Time

If Avon made direct sales trendy among women, another company made it trendy among *trendy* women: Tupperware.

That was all thanks to a woman you've probably never heard of: Brownie Wise. She was truly a gal after my own heart: a single mother from Detroit with heaps of charisma and impeccable personal style, which would become the hallmark of all early Tupperware ladies. She played the saxophone. She was an executive at an aeronautics company. She wrote a sort of Dear Abby–like advice column for the local paper. When she was at home, she'd fearlessly answer the door to salesmen, such as the one from Stanley Home Products who swung by her Detroit home in 1947.

Stanley Home Products was owned by Frank Stanley Beveridge and was the first company to have great success with the party model of selling, in which company representatives would host gatherings of potential customers at someone's home, offer them hors d'oeuvres and drinks, and entice them to buy products. Beveridge sold boring household items such as mops, brooms, and brushes. One day, a Stanley Home Products salesman[17] knocked on Wise's door and, according to her, flubbed the pitch so badly—it was just a real stinker—that Wise got to thinking she'd be *great at this job*. After all, becoming a sharp-dressed aeronautical-engineering executive and saxophonist was a breeze. So she applied for that man's position and got it.

Mind you, this was just after World War II, a period when women were hustling like crazy to pay the bills. Thanks to their efforts during the war when the men who previously filled "manly" positions had been sent overseas, women were starting to gain partial acceptance as a fundamental part of the workforce. It only took Wise a year to become a regional rep at Stanley Home Products, running the sales force in southeast Michigan and Ohio.

One year after she began working there, she and her team were invited to the company headquarters in Massachusetts. During the visit, Wise, eager to continue moving up the ranks, got some face time with the company executives, who told her to chill on her ambitions. "Management is no place for a woman," they said. She went home, rightfully pissed.[18]

That's when a guy on her sales team, a teenager named Gary MacDonald, introduced her to this weird new product he'd found at a department store: the Tupperware Wonder Bowl. It was not sold by Stanley Home Products, or anyone else of note.

Launched in 1946, Tupperware is one of *the* most iconic MLMs of all time, and the brand is basically synonymous with the idea of the MLM sales party. Tupperware and its related storage-container products are so ubiquitous today that it's easy to forget that, when the original Tupperware bowl was introduced, it was a truly strange, new product, and it took a while to catch on. Plastics were relatively new in the 1940s, and most families stored food in glass or ceramic containers, which were heavy, broke easily, and were not all that great at, you know, storing food. Tupperware was the latest and most successful product in a long string of inventions by an enterprising man named Earl . . . wait for it . . . Tupper.

Tupper started out as a tree surgeon—someone who tries to save dying greenery—but that didn't make him a ton of money, so he began to apply for patents left and right. He was an inventor, which was an actual job title dudes aspired to a hundred years ago. He patented an ice cream cone with a wide rim to catch the drips. He made something called a Dagger Comb, which was a comb meant to easily attach to swimsuits for God knows why? Some of his inventions were flat-out nonsense, such as a boat powered by fish.

Then, in the late 1930s, Tupper went to work for Du-Pont, which was at the cutting edge of plastics innovation.[19] In 1936, polyethylene was patented, and everyone in plastics was pumped, trying to figure out what this new compound could do. Today, we use it to make such things as plastic bags (that's what the *PE* printed on them stands for). Back then, most engineers were looking for ways to strengthen this new substance. Not Earl Tupper. He wanted to make it weaker. Bendier. More pliable. So he added polypropylene and polystyrene and voilà! Tupper perfected the formula for his groundbreaking plastic and in 1946[20] launched Tupperware.

Homemakers just loved the idea of switching from glass storage containers to ones that could never, without a lot of effort, make their children bleed or cause a blood-colored Jell-O stain on the carpet. There were already melamine and hard plastic bowls, but Tupper added pliability and a lid that, when closed correctly, made a burping sound signaling an airtight seal. (You can thank Earl Tupper for that overflowing cupboard or drawer full of Tupperware knockoffs and successors.)

His invention was revolutionary, and that's not hyperbole. Suddenly food was more portable and lasted longer and food containers were safer. Tupperware launched a line of bowls to much critical acclaim, with engineers and designers and press around the country oohing and aahing at what he'd created. But none of the hype translated into sales. So what was the issue? Well, the product was *too* new, and people didn't understand how it should work without seeing the bowls and lids in action.

This dilemma is something MLMs often use to justify why their products are sold through a pyramid structure and not in stores: people need to be taught, in person, one-on-one, how to use novel inventions. If MLMs were the only way to do that, there would be no trade shows, and no one giving out free samples at Costco or the fair. You've probably gotten an email or a flyer with a coupon for some meal-kit company, with some variation of the following promise: "Get four free meals today and only pay shipping!" Companies such as HelloFresh and Blue Apron know that, until you've gotten your hands on a meal kit, it's hard to tell if it would be something you'd like to pay for, so they build these free try-before-you-buy meals into their marketing budgets. MLMs choose *not* to market their products this way because every opportunity to sell goods to the sellers of the goods is seen as a good thing. There are no free lunches in MLMs.

Tupper didn't start out thinking he'd go the MLM route. He first tried going straight to retail, something the sharks on *Shark Tank* will readily tell you is nearly impossible in a field as packed as home goods. But this was post–World War II, when homemaking was all the rage, along with "modern conveniences" such as microwave ovens. People were buying houses in the suburbs through ads in magazines and imagining futures where robots ran the kitchen, so Tupper assumed they would be all over this new Tupperware. Tupper spent many hours standing in the housewares section of department stores demonstrating the burp, but sales remained stagnant,[21] and I think I know why. Tupper was kind of a dud (sorry, Earl). Tupper was no ShamWow guy and couldn't hold a candle to Billy Mays (RIP). He looked like Dan Akroyd with none of the humor or charm. Enter the effervescent Brownie Wise.

After her salesman at Stanley Home Products tipped her to the Tupperware Wonder Bowl, Wise bought a bunch of them wholesale and had her team hawk them alongside Stanley products to see what would happen. She wasn't the only one in the country doing this; dozens of sales organizations tried adding Tupperware to their offerings, but Wise brought a special sauce to her operation that no one else could compete with. Instead of going door-to-door selling to individuals, she teamed up with local "hostesses"—women who would offer up their living rooms or backyards as event spaces—and invited potential bowl buyers for a casual gathering where Wise or one of her team of reps would demonstrate products using techniques she'd picked up from her time at Stanley. This was not some boring dude in a suit explaining the material makeup of the plastic or the technology that made the bowls so innovative. This was a stylish woman talking to other women and having a great time doing it.

In 1949, Tupper was looking at his books and noticed the skyrocketing sales coming out of Michigan.[22] That year Wise, as an unofficial distributor, had ordered $86,407.15 worth of Tupperware, wholesale. That's nearly $1 million in today's dollars. Tupper was floored and sent a representative to her home to find out what she was doing to move so much product, and that's when she told the company about her parties. On the spot, the company asked her to become an official Tupperware distributor, but the hitch was that she'd need to move to Florida. Not a problem. Wise and her young son gleefully headed for the Sunshine State, and many of her top sellers in icy Michigan came right along with them. In May of 1950,[23] Wise opened her first Tupperware business in Hollywood, Florida. She began recruiting locals straightaway and wrote up a training manual that focused heavily on what she called Patio Parties.

"The buying spirit is *contagious*," the plan read. "It is a proven fact that you will sell more to a group of 15 women AS A GROUP than you will sell to them individually. This is the essence of the Patio Party Plan." Distributors were to offer the hostess a free piece of Tupperware, $1.50 in cash for every additional party that was booked in another home during her party, as well as 5 percent of the total proceeds from any sales.[24] To make the parties even more appealing, Wise reached into her own closet to find dresses and accessories that she could raffle off to the assembled guests. She also instructed her reps to fill the Tupperware bowls with food and *throw* them around during parties so women could see how airtight and durable they were. This strategy led to her slogan "They don't break, they bounce!"

The parties were so lively, guests often described them as being more like social events than sales pitches. "Women didn't have a car to get around anywhere, so we sat home all day and we took care of our kids," said former Tupperware sales rep Mary Siriani in an interview with the PBS show *American Experience*. "A Tupperware party was the social function; it was the way to get away from the kids for a few hours during the week." Wise began assembling starter kits that she sold for $35 to women who wanted to do what she was doing, and the party plan was up and running.

The Patio Party Plan was such a runaway success that Earl Tupper asked Wise to become his vice president. It was then that she began formulating the criteria for those who would become Tupperware ladies. Wise came up with a short list of qualifications for the role, including "she must have a real need to earn at least $50 a week" and "if she is married, her husband must be willing to see her give several evenings a week to our work." [25] Don't you just love a divorcée?

To further spur growth, Wise encouraged existing reps to actively recruit others into the fold. "She would say, 'Now how many dealers have you recruited a month, Mary?'" Siriani said. "'Wouldn't it be wonderful'—and she squeezed your hand and said, 'if it would be eight or ten? Wouldn't that be nice?'" [26] The company, under Wise's direction, taught reps specific tactics to identify and attract potential recruits, such as walking them through how the extra income could help them afford a new appliance or piece of furniture, or, in some cases, resorting to straight-out flattery.

"At a party, I'd see a lady who seemed to be very enthusiastic, she seemed to like people, she was a bubbly type person," said another former salesperson, Anna Tate. "And I would say to her, 'You know, I don't know if you've ever thought about doing any work outside your home. I bet you would be a terrific Tupperware lady.'" [27]

Given the status of women in the 1950s, it's no wonder a simple compliment like this could win someone over. Many of these ladies may have tasted the independence that comes from earning one's own money, either in jobs they had prior to getting married or in work they'd done outside the home while the men were off at war. Many women had earned degrees only to set aside whatever skills, knowledge, or interests they had nurtured when they said "I do." Women such as my great-grandmother Maxine were no doubt yearning for a way to feel productive and independent, to prove they could do more than change diapers and make a good pot roast—to show off a little and assert their individuality and intelligence.

The enthusiastic encouragement didn't stop once a woman joined Tupperware. Wise spent unbelievable energy motivating and encouraging her workforce. She had a saying: "You build the people, and they'll build the business," and she lived it every chance she got.[28] She traveled all over the country—150,000 miles a year, supposedly—to meet her reps and distributors in person and shake their hands. And it's impossible to find a photo of Wise in which she isn't impeccably put together. I mean, she was stunning. She wore fit-and-flare dresses, the classic cut of the day. I regularly get Wise and Vera-Ellen, one of the stars of *White Christmas*, confused in my head—petite blondes with perfectly coiffed hair and waists so tiny one wonders how they could breathe, let alone remain charming and active. Charm was Wise's magic power.

She loved to shine her light upon others. Wise published a monthly newsletter, *Tupperware Sparks*, in which she gave shout-outs to her top sellers. "Most people only had their name in the paper when they graduated from high school or when they got married, or when they'd die," said former Tupperware PR person Pat Tahaney. "And I think that she drew on all aspects of that to create a feeling in these people that they were a queen, that they were special, that they were somebody different." [29]

Over the next few years, with Wise in the lead, business boomed, but she did experience her fair share of disappointments. Tupper had been slow to shut down other Tupperware distributors in her area when she first moved to Florida, and two years in, he had yet to make good on a promise to remove Tupperware from store shelves—exclusivity being a key selling point in Wise's promotion. She rallied the troops, some of her big-time male distributors, and together they diplomatically told Tupper it was now or never. He conceded and the company went completely direct to consumer. In 1952, distributors ordered more than $2 million worth of product.

Based off this success, Tupperware built an office for Wise in Florida, a headquarters the size of an airplane hangar.[30] The company also bought her a luxury home with hundreds of feet of frontage on a lake and an indoor swimming pool. For her fortieth birthday, Tupper sent her a palomino horse to get her around the property. Wise was making $30,000 per year as an executive. That's $700,000 in today's money, which is a lot, but it does make you wonder: If she was being paid that much, why the pony and the house and all that? Was this business so profitable that Tupper didn't want to let Wise in on it?

Maybe because of the horse and the lake, or maybe just because she was fabulous, Wise seems to have gotten a little swept up in her own cult of personality. She was the first woman to appear on the cover of *Business Week*. In 1956, she set to work on a motivational book called *Best Wishes, Brownie Wise* and left the company for the better part of a year to go on a promotional tour for the book. These moves didn't sit well with Tupper, who also didn't appreciate how Wise used the book and the tour to take credit for most of Tupperware's success. Things came to a head in 1957 during the company's annual jubilee party for top sellers, an event Wise had conceived of three years prior.

She'd invited hundreds of guests to a tiny island in a lake near Kissimmee, Florida, and planned a weekend full of international-themed feasts. There were tiki bars and exotic fare, raffles, and motivational speakers. Wise spent a lot time thinking about the optics, how to make the place look as special as she wanted attendees to feel. But a surprise storm came along to test her. Wise had failed to consider the logistics of transporting her guests safely to and from the island during such an event. The storm sent the ferries she had hired careening into one another, stranding many of the hundreds of attendees, and Wise panicked. It was the Fyre Fest of MLMs. Rather than deploy her generally cheerful disposition and knack for event planning to manage the crisis and put people at ease, Wise fled the island the first chance she got, leaving much of her flock to fend for themselves. This may not have been the catalyst for what came next, but it was certainly a harbinger of doom.

Shortly after the botched jubilee, the company's annual report came out. For the first time, Tupperware experienced a sales slump, with only 20 percent annual growth instead of the year-over-year doubling of profit it had come to expect thanks to Wise's innovations. Wise took the fall.

Tupper accused her of being distracted with self-promotion as an author and semi-celebrity. Wise blamed herself for not focusing on incentivizing those lowest in the food chain at the company, the folks on the ground moving product. All this focus on rewarding top earners left over twenty thousand Tupperware ladies wondering if they mattered to the company at all. Wise admitted to this oversight in a letter to Tupper: "We discounted the personal (and basically human) needs of all distributors. We simply forgot."

In January 1958, Wise was canned by the board of directors and offered a lower position in the company. She declined and sued the company for "blacklisting" her in the sales world. Eventually the suit was settled for $30,000. Tupper sold the company the next year for $16 million.

*   *   *

Today, most MLMs lead with the idea that they exist so women can enjoy more freedom, both financially and for time with their families; time they can dedicate toward their wifely or motherly duties. Or, heck, maybe they can be so successful they don't even *need* a man. Wise sure proved that, but did she? Years of being a #bossbabe ended with a small severance package. Brownie Wise never earned equity in the company she catalyzed.

Part-time entrepreneurship remains a core promise of most modern-day MLM brands—including Avon, which entices twenty-first-century women, "Be a beauty influencer, skin care expert, whatever-your-passion entrepreneur, from home or on the go, live or virtually." [31] Amway promises, "Be in business for yourself, but never by yourself." [32] With LuLaRoe, you can "become a fashion entrepreneur" and "start your own business with the flexibility to reach *your* goals on *your* schedule." [33]

There's just one problem: Avon ladies, or any independent contractors for multi-level-marketing companies, are not entrepreneurs in any true sense of the word. They don't have upfront risk that most business owners do (this is *also* part of the pitch to join one), but they also don't have the same potential for rewards because these salespeople don't control anything except their own sales efforts. They don't own the product they're selling or any intellectual property. They don't set their own prices or salaries, and they are often bound by strict rules outlined in their contract governing how they can market and sell their products. And since they are independent contractors, which means technically they work for themselves and not the company, they lack even the basic protections afforded to employees at a typical corporation—such as a guaranteed salary, benefits, and worker's rights afforded most employees under the law. This model lies at the far end of the spectrum of capitalist exploitation, where the workers have their bootstraps and not much else.

Still, the *idea* of making money without having to show up to an office every day, or at all, is fundamentally appealing, especially among women with relatively few opportunities to earn their own income and with obligations to the unpaid labors of home.

3

Original Huksters

I t would be no exaggeration to say that without Carl Rehnborg, there would perhaps *be* no MLMs. No Arbonne or
Herbalife or Scentsy. No Pure Romance. But Carl didn't intend for any of this to happen. He just wanted to make a
name for himself and a potion that would bring good health
to the masses. Carl Rehnborg and his magical, mystical vitamin company, Nutrilite. If that name sounds familiar, it's
because Nutrilite is still being sold through one of the world's
largest MLMs today: Amway.

As with many MLM-founder stories, it's pretty much
impossible to divorce reality from mythmaking because the
narrative is always shaped by those closest to the subject—in

Carl's case that person is his son Sam. In 2009, on the seventieth anniversary of Nutrilite's founding, Sam published a gushing hagiography of his late father, entitled *The Nutrilite Story: Past, Present, Future.* Physically, the book is giant. It measures nine-by-nine inches and has nearly seven hundred pages of overly detailed yet often chronologically confused anecdotes from Carl's fascinating (some might say bizarre) life as one of America's most influential businessmen you've never heard of.

Born in June 1887 in St. Augustine, Florida, to Swedish immigrants, Carl spent the first few decades of his life consumed by wanderlust, and particularly an obsession with China. He was far from alone. The lure of the Far East is what brought Europeans to North America in the first place, and the pull of the ocean that connected the Occident and the Orient fueled expansion of the United States to the west.[1] The Mexican-American War was partially rooted in the U.S. government's desire to control California's port cities and, thus, access to Asian markets and labor.[2] That labor force from Asia eventually built the transcontinental railroad. Around the turn of the nineteenth century, obsession morphed into fetishization. During the Victorian era, "orientalism" took hold in America. Asian art, food, religion—all of Asian culture was co-opted by white Americans in their homes, their silent films, their tea gardens. This was the world Carl earnestly, and naively, fantasized about becoming a part of.

In 1906, when Carl was nineteen, his family moved again,

to Pinehurst, North Carolina, a village best known for its famous golf resort and home to some of America's wealthiest families. After a financially unpredictable nomadic childhood, Carl suddenly found himself living among Mellons and Morgans, DuPonts and Rockefellers. In an effort to fit in, Carl began dressing differently from how he had as a vagabond kid, preferring starched suits and perfectly shined shoes. "My father was actively nurturing a dashing persona," Sam writes of his dad's sartorial choices.[3]

In awe of the wealth and status of these new neighbors, Carl did what any normal American teenager would do—he came up with a list of twenty-six rules to help him comport himself successfully, especially around women. According to Sam, Carl was a "dashing" young man who "in conversation made women feel special," but apparently Carl thought he needed a little direction. Rule 17: "Make up to the little sisters and all small girls. You may be able to lord over them when they are ten and you are twenty, but someday when they are twenty and you are thirty, the tables will be turned—and they don't forget!" Rule 25: "Don't be timid about 'butting-in' at a ball. No girl in this world was ever annoyed because a man made her look popular." I mean, you gotta admit he was onto something.

The rules worked, as Carl soon began to have time for little else than wooing receptive women (and their little sisters?) throughout the area. Carl took a job helping his father establish distribution outlets for the family jewelry business, but Carl's immaturity prevented him from succeeding. "He worked hard by his own account," Sam writes. "But it seemed to take second place to his passions for socializing, dancing, and making sales rounds riding his unicycle."

Carl and his father agreed that Carl should put his energy toward something else. So Carl quit and took a job as a supervisor at a garter and corset manufacturer, but was fired after just two weeks, allegedly because "his amiable style failed to motivate the crew." But you gotta admit young Carl sounds like a pretty chill hang.

Carl set his sights on New York City, originally determined to make it big on Broadway, but eventually he settled for a position in the jewelry-design program at the Pratt Institute in Brooklyn, where, for a time, he thought he might follow in his father's footsteps and get into the jewelry business. Carl never completed the program, but he did meet a woman named Hester, a young "heiress" (to what fortune Sam does not say) from Massachusetts who shared Carl's fascination with the Far East and, at least for a few years, seemed perfectly content dating a dreamer with a knack for starting things he couldn't finish.

After leaving Pratt without a degree and giving up his jewelry-making ambitions, Carl took a series of odd jobs, including inventing a waterproof-and-fireproof flooring material that didn't perform well at either,[4] operating a streetcar in South Carolina, and working as a copy editor for a local newspaper. He made two more failed attempts at college, during which he penned an essay for an English class titled "Is Conformity Desirable?":

> We have to be concerned consciously and for all our lives with creating, from the materials of the universe which came into our possession, the thoughts and things only we can create because we happen to be our individual selves, unlike any other self anywhere.

The idea of American individualism and exceptionalism enchanted Carl very early on. By age twenty-seven, Carl had little to show for his life, except probably a lot of fun memories. He was a failed inventor, failed salesperson, and a failed student. His relationship with Hester went cold when he moved South, so you can add failed lover to the list. But that didn't stop him from dreaming big. Inspired by the stories of rugged frontiersmen such as Jack London, men who could prosper in conquering the wilderness, Carl decided to venture West to join the Alaska gold rush. By the time he arrived in Seattle, he found out the Klondike gold rush had ended fifteen years prior and nothing was left in them thar hills. But he'd maintained his captivation with China, which was now closer than ever. While in Seattle, Carl learned about the fortunes people were making ever since international trade agreements had opened up the ports between China and the United States a few decades prior. He decided to seek work overseas, headed back to New York, and applied for a job with Standard Oil's Chinese division. It is unclear how he—with no experience, credentials, or education—got the job, but given that this was America in 1915 and he was a well-dressed mediocre white guy with a knack for hanging out and riding unicycles, it would probably have been a breeze for him to get an entry-level international sales job at any of the world's largest corporations.

The point is, he got the job and soon found himself on a steamer to China, his dream of exploring Asia finally realized. Once there, he reached out to Hester, no doubt knowing how envious she would be that he was now living in the country they'd swooned over together. His contract with Standard Oil explicitly required him to remain single for the three years he was there, but Carl didn't care. He continued to woo Hester, and it worked. He married Hester, lost his job, then moved her to China to live with him while he figured out his next step. This time it would be right up his alley: hawking furs and leathers and other imported American specialty items in communities surrounding Shanghai.

As part of the traveling-salesman lifestyle, Carl got up close and personal with the residents of Shanghai and the surrounding areas, just as he'd always envisioned. He'd walk all day, in and out of neighborhoods, hauling a cart full of goods or, between shipments, an order sheet. On these walks, one thing stuck out to him: some of the ailments people had in China were new to him. One of the most common was beriberi, which is caused by a lack of thiamine and can lead to swollen limbs, memory loss, paralysis, and even death. Carl noticed that, strangely, the disease seemed to afflict only wealthy city dwellers, while poorer rural residents were spared. He wondered, Did it have anything to do with their diet?

Despite his lack of any medical, nutritional, or scientific training, his suspicions would be proven correct. The husks of brown rice are rich in thiamine, but white rice—which was at that time literally and figuratively more refined—is processed to remove the husks so it lacks this important nutrient. Since urbanites tended to favor the processed white rice, they weren't getting enough thiamine in their diet and were more prone to beriberi. According to Sam's telling, Carl continued to hypothesize about the connections between diet and the diseases he observed throughout China. "He could see children with bowed legs and old women hunched over like question marks, their bones as brittle as dried twigs," Sam writes.

For a brief time Hester and Carl returned to the United States, where Hester gave birth to their first child, Sam's older brother, Ned. Carl kept working for the trading company, this time hustling leather to Mexico and Texas, while his wife stayed with her well-to-do family in Boston. Not long after, he quit his job (shocker), but got a new one at a shipbuilding company in Texas. Carl just continued to fail sideways. While in Texas, he contracted the Spanish flu and was hospitalized.[5] As Carl convalesced and fever-dreamed, his thoughts drifted back to all those "hunched over" people he'd ogled in China. "Drawing from his own childhood and the emphasis his family placed on drinking milk, he wondered if their conditions could be alleviated by drinking milk, which was known to contain calcium, an important mineral for strong bones. Were they getting enough calcium in their diet?"

A light bulb went off. Once out of the hospital, Carl contacted Carnation Milk and asked if he could become an overseas sales rep for *them* because, clearly, the Chinese needed more calcium to fortify their bones, and what better way to get calcium than through good old-fashioned milk? Carnation said, yes, ah-no-duh. But before he left the States, Carnation had Carl visit some of their farms as part of his training. At these dairy farms Carl learned that, according to Carnation employees, cows that grazed on a steady diet of alfalfa produced the best milk. He stuck the notion "alfalfa = healthy" in his mind's back pocket. The Rehnborgs returned to Shanghai, and Carl began setting up his network of sales associates to move canned milk through the vast countryside.

He started hanging out with Chinese alchemists and herbalists, finally pursuing some real education around his new passions: diet and nutrition. The plants he was introduced to reminded him of his childhood when his mother would give him teas and tinctures made from various boiled roots to ease aches and pains. He learned that in traditional Chinese medicine, ginger was used for indigestion, yam ameliorated depression, and a special fish-and-egg soup was the best cure for menstrual cramps.

Soon, Carl began making his own health tinctures, hopeful that he could come up with some supercharged wellness concoction that would stave off all sorts of diseases without requiring people to completely change their diets. Vitamins were just barely being studied by scientists and wouldn't be introduced to the world for many years. So, going on instinct, Carl ground bones and shells for their minerals and used the powder as a condiment. He left the skins on everything he cooked in case the nutrients were held there. He even put rusty nails in tea, believing they would deliver much-needed iron. According to his family, he ruined the taste of their home-cooked meals as they became his unwitting guinea pigs.

As much fun as he was having in the kitchen, Carl became discouraged by the slow pace of his milk distribution outlet. It just wasn't taking off the way he and Carnation had hoped. Reps reported that no one liked the taste and that people were even getting sick from canned milk. The hole in the market that Carnation thought it could fill was because the Chinese have a genetic predisposition to lactose intolerance and have trouble digesting dairy. Carl had to go back to the drawing board.

One thing I'll say for Carl Rehnborg: for someone who excelled at quitting, he sure kept putting himself out there. After being forced to return, once again, to the States penniless and dejected, Carl being Carl probably thought, "Hmm . . . what's something I haven't seen in China that I could make money selling in China because I really just feel like I need to live in China for some reason?" This time he settled on personal hygiene products and turned to Colgate. As the story goes, he hopped a train to Jersey City, New Jersey, home of the company headquarters, walked into Harry Colgate's office, and got a job as the company's independent sales representative for China. This fuckin' guy. Once again gainfully employed, he convinced Hester and their now three children, including his biographer, Sam, to return with him and, as a consolation, promised his wife a few more servants and a fancier house in a French expat neighborhood. She accepted the invitation. This was Shanghai, 1924.

Just as he was experiencing his first real success, a nationalist movement took root in China after the Treaty of Versailles awarded Chinese lands that had been surrendered to the Germans during World War I to Japan instead of returning them to China. Student protests led to the formation of the Chinese Communist Party, and in the mid-1920s its leaders began taking over major cities. There was *a lot* of civil unrest. The Rehnborgs' Shanghai neighborhood became a de facto refugee settlement as fighting spread across the country and Western businesses pulled out of the territory. Carl lost his contract with Colgate. Rather than running from the chaos around him, Carl saw this as an opportunity. He began working part-time as a liaison between foreign expatriates and communist insurgents, but mostly went around gathering greens and other materials to cook up health drinks for the legions of malnourished people now flooding the city. In them, he found willing, hungry test subjects and encouragement in his pursuit of concocting a bone, rusty-nail, or alfalfa tonic for the world's infirm.

Maybe it was the constant back-and-forth travel. Maybe it was living in a foreign country during a cultural uprising. Maybe she just preferred her rusty nails with Scotch and Drambuie. Whatever the case, in March 1927 Hester got fed up with Carl. She and the children moved back to Massachusetts and Hester filed for divorce.

About a month later, Carl gave up, too. Civil war loomed, his career wasn't panning out, and he was lonely. With no family, no job, and just $24 to his name, Carl sent a wire to Colgate, begging his old employer for a ticket home. Once again, they couldn't say no, and he boarded a ship for the United States on June 24, just a month and a half before war broke out. He could have gone back East to be with his family like a responsible guy, sure, but instead he settled in Southern California—land of dreams and misguided ambition. It would take him four years to plan a trip to Massachusetts to visit his children, though his son Sam has spun the story more favorably: "In many of the great 'vision quest' legends worldwide, the would-be-warrior must undergo a season of testing in the desert."

Carl spent his vision quest working odd jobs: babysitting, shift-managing at a hospital, and mining sodium out in the Mojave Desert. Then one day Carl met a woman named Mildred, fourteen years his junior, while driving through Bakersfield. That's all the details we have about that. But with Hester and the kids out of sight, Carl and Mildred engaged in a whirlwind romance. They were married and expecting a baby within a year. Then tragedy struck. Mildred started complaining of stomach pain and was diagnosed with appendicitis quite far into the pregnancy. Although the emergency surgery was successful, she later developed sepsis and lost the baby. Days later, at the age of thirty-one, Mildred succumbed as well.

Alfalfa Ambition

After the news of Mildred's death reached Hester up in Boston, a young woman named Evie who babysat for members of Hester's family either lost her mind or . . . no, that's all I got. When Evie heard that Carl—widower and abandoner of children—was suddenly single, she hopped on a train to California in the hope of becoming the third Mrs. Rehnborg. Who does that!? And guess what? Carl said sure.

With Evie's obvious blind adoration, Carl could finally focus on his vitamin thingamabob without judgment. The newlyweds settled on Balboa Island in Orange County, California, and Carl set up a laboratory in their kitchen. He began experimenting, specifically this time, with ways to make a nutritional supplement out of his beloved alfalfa.

It stank. The laboratory, that is. The smell of alfalfa cooking was apparently so pungent that neighbors started complaining to authorities and the Rehnborgs were forced to leave the island. No matter. They moved and Carl continued tinkering in their next house and in 1936 founded California Vitamin, Inc., later renamed Nutrilite.

For perhaps the first time in his life, Carl's timing was impeccable. Remember how vitamins were just becoming a thing when Carl was working in China? That's because scientists around the world simultaneously started having the same hunches as Carl: similar to how those new things called germs worked, what if there were components of food that kept us from getting sick or, even better, made us healthier? What if we could use the ingredients found naturally in food as medicine? Industrialization brought with it many hidden dangers to our health, among them processed and preserved foods.

These innovations allowed more people to access affordable food, but stripped the food of nutrition.

In 1912, a Polish scientist named Casimir Funk had isolated thiamine, or vitamin B_1, which was necessary to prevent beriberi, the disease whose effects Carl had witnessed firsthand in China. I include Funk here because I like his name. His discovery was a first in the field. He came up with the portmanteau *vitamin*, *vita* being Latin for "life"[6] and *amine* for "amino acids," which Funk wrongly assumed were part of vitamins. Others argued for *food hormone* and *accessory food factor*, to no avail.[7] Next came the discoveries by other scientists around the world of more B vitamins as well as vitamins A and D. In 1922, a UC Berkeley lab discovered vitamin E in green vegetables. During the late 1920s through the 1930s, all kinds of researchers began publishing op-eds and pamphlets extolling the virtues of vitamins. But around the time Carl joined the fray, most of these people were still seen as quacks. During the Great Depression, the public just wanted food, period. Plus the science just wasn't there yet. But a few people, including Carl, saw these discoveries as the future of human health, and what would become the massive vitamin and supplement market slowly began to emerge.

Early on, in 1929, the Food and Drug Administration (FDA) got wind of this craze and sent out a notice to Americans to be wary of any products being sold as a "vitamin." They were not, the FDA warned, cure-alls and could never replace a healthy diet of real foods. But no one could argue that the rapid rise in popularity of cheap, shelf-stable processed foods, such as bleached flour and white sugar, had *something* to do with declining health during and after the Great Depression. Milling flour removes most of its naturally occurring B_1, and at that time flour made up 25 percent of the U.S. diet.[8] So what turned the tide? Well, money. Food manufacturers in the late 1930s and early '40s saw these new discoveries as a potential selling point: your food is processed, but now we can put back what we took with special compounds you can't see or taste! Thus fortified foods such as milk, flour, and cereals were born and proved to be extremely popular during a time when folks greatly feared being malnourished.

The truth of vitamins is this: Humans only need thirteen of them. One, vitamin D, we can make ourselves, but the rest we have to ingest. This discovery took decades and many teams of scientists, but upon Casimir Funk's discovery, researchers around the world started digging further into the causal relationships between diet and illness. By Carl's time, the scientific community had solidly established that we needed vitamins, and suddenly everyone wanted more of them, not just the thirteen. Surely that's not *all* we need, right? Or so the thinking went. That's what Carl and thousands of others thought and *still* think to this day.

Think about that for a moment. For eons, humans roamed the earth eating what was available and even sometimes delicious, but believed that sickness had nothing to do with what they consumed. Instead, ailments were believed to be caused by gods, or a bad attitude, or a witch's curse. Suddenly, with germ theory and vitamins, well-being had a moral element. That is, a lack of or presence of invisible but very real substances in one's body could manifest in negative outward signs. You'd have to be pretty ignorant to be in poor health, so wellness became a marker of intelligence and privilege.

In 1939, Carl rebranded the California Vitamin company to a name that didn't include the word *vitamin* because who knew what the next big nutritional discovery would be called? He decided on the vague but scientific-sounding *Nutrilite* and began marketing his first products. One regimen called XX and pronounced "double x" sold for $20 (roughly $220 in today's money) for a one-month supply. XX was a trio of supplements, including an oil containing fat-soluble vitamins, a capsule with plant concentrates, and a mineral tablet meant to be taken once a day. Nothing in this supplement was inherently harmful, but little science backed up what Carl claimed it *did* do. No one was more confused about how to handle this than what was then called the federal Food, Drug, and Insecticide Administration.

Welcome to the Jungle

Back in 1906, Congress passed the Food and Drug Act in response to the publication of Upton Sinclair's *The Jungle*. Set in Chicago's meatpacking district, *The Jungle* shocked readers with its raw descriptions of the horrific, unsanitary, and unregulated conditions from which Americans' Sunday roasts originated. The act gave the government oversight of the purity of foods and drugs in an effort to prevent contamination, fraud, and tampering. Under this act, you could no longer market sawdust as flour or peddle products that had been knowingly altered or were infested with vermin. What the act did *not* do, though, was prevent companies from making spurious claims about the health benefits of their products. It was still perfectly legal to sell snake oil as long as that snake oil wasn't *known* to have killed anyone and you didn't lie about what was in it. A spate of lawsuits followed, with individuals claiming products had harmed them and companies alleging they were unfairly regulated. One case went all the way to the Supreme Court in 1914, which decided that adding nitrite to flour wasn't illegal until it was proven that nitrite was bad. Whether nitrite is bad is still being debated over one hundred years later, but the consensus seems to be it's bad in high quantities.

But something definitive did happen around this time that led to the regulatory system we still use today to help ensure what we're ingesting isn't going to kill us: the 1937 sulfanil-amide disaster.[9] Originally developed in tablet form, sulfanil-amide had long been used to treat strep throat, but when the pharmaceutical company Massengill created a sulfanilamide syrup for children, it used diethylene glycol, the sweet-tasting compound found in antifreeze, as a liquid suspension. The company tested its new Elixir of Sulfanilamide for taste, color, and fragrance but not for safety. In just two months, 107 people (mostly children) died after taking the elixir, and the medical community, government, and general public were outraged. Under the 1906 law, the government had little authority to go after Massengill or to remove the drug from the market because, technically, the company hadn't done anything illegal by selling a toxic product. The government did, however, charge the company with "misbranding," alleg-ing the term *elixir* implied the substance contained alcohol, which it did not.

FDA commissioner Walter Campbell called for more oversight and regulation of drugs. "These unfortunate oc-currences may be expected to continue because new and relatively untried drug preparations are being manufactured almost daily at the whim of the individual manufacturer, and the damage to public health cannot accurately be esti-mated," he declared. "The only remedy for such a situation is the enactment by Congress of an adequate and compre-hensive national Food and Drugs Act which will require that all medicines placed upon the market shall be safe under the directions for use." [10]

Finally, after years of hemming and hawing about how to properly regulate the drug market, the government passed the 1938 federal Food, Drug, and Cosmetic Act,[11] which required proper ingredient listings, directions for use, and testing for safety and efficacy and established a legal precedent by which people who had been harmed, or the government itself, could hold these companies accountable for damages. Prior to this, people were still using arsenic in makeup, eyelash dyes were blinding women, and people were sold energy drinks that contained radium, which leads to a slow, painful death by radiation. Luckily for Carl and his ilk, the act failed to clearly define whether vitamins and supplements should be considered foods or drugs and therefore be subject to the same regulations as those classes, or whether they were something else entirely. That meant that things in Carl's realm were okeydokey, for now.

The Plan

The early twentieth century saw rapid urbanization and mass production, which led to the proliferation of retail outlets in areas where once there weren't any. People who lived on farms no longer had to wait for the traveling salesman to show up on his buggy; they could drive to town and fill their trunks with a variety of goods. But with vitamins still so new to the market, it wasn't yet standard to see them on store shelves, so Carl decided to release his line the old-fashioned way: door-to-door, or at least something like it. The thinking was that since vitamins were so novel, it would be best to have a representative explain the benefits to customers in person. Today, many consumers take vitamins and supplements habitually, but back in the forties and fifties, they weren't a regular part of people's diets—folks were still assuming (often correctly) that they could get all the vitamins they needed from foods. Carl wanted to convince them otherwise and sell them the solution.

Before he hit the market, though, Carl gifted his supplements to his friends and acquaintances in exchange for their feedback. No one died. Now Carl was off to the races. From the guinea pigs who reported liking Carl's concoctions, he began recruiting folks to make up his team of salespeople and offered them a small kickback for referring other people to become sales reps as well. This approach was just a commission-based sales model, one that you see in lots of legitimate businesses, with a onetime bonus for bringing in new talent. But that wouldn't last long for Carl.

One day in, an ever-curious Carl attended a sales seminar run by Dale Carnegie, who wrote *How to Win Friends and Influence People* and one of the forefathers of the modern motivational-psychology and self-help movement. Carnegie's actual name was Carnagey, until he changed it to sound more like Andrew Carnegie, the industrialist, steel tycoon, and bazillionaire. Under this new, fancier moniker, Dale Carnegie pioneered sales tactics we now take for granted, such as saying a potential customer's name a bunch while you chat, or talking "in terms of the other person's interest"—basically ways to convince people that they can trust you and want what you're selling. Whether or not he learned something, Carl felt the seminar would be a good place to recruit people who could help him rapidly expand, and he was right. While there, he met a psychologist and radio personality named William Casselberry and convinced him to join Nutrilite. Casselberry brought along his business partner, Lee Mytinger, and the two set up a new, separate company that would exclusively market and distribute Nutrilite products. Carl remained head of Nutrilite and oversaw research, development, and manufacturing. He was relieved to be able to focus on his favorite parts of the business while true businessmen focused on the rest.

In marketing acumen, William Casselberry was an expert in what would later be referred to as neurolinguistic programming, or NLP, a pseudoscience that claims that the way you think and speak, both to yourself and others, can allow you to achieve optimal success in life. Or something? I dunno, a lot of cult leaders including Keith Raniere of NXIVM love it, if that tells you anything. Casselberry also wrote a book called *How to Use Psychology in Everyday Living.*

So, based on this "knowledge" of human behavior, Casselberry and Mytinger revamped Nutrilite's entire way of doing business in 1941.[12] First, they declared the vitamins should be sold through a subscription program. Not *pre*scription, subscription: buyers would be urged to sign up for automatic monthly shipments, because how else would they have enough supply to see the benefits of the product? These subscriptions, like most, were inconvenient to cancel. They also introduced a new policy that allowed distributors to earn a 2 percent bonus for each person they recruited into the organization, in addition to the 35 percent commission they were making on all of their personal sales.[13] Anyone could join, but people's success would depend on whether they proved to be just a "potentate," a "high potentate," or, best of all, an "exalted potentate." *Potentate* literally means "ruler," especially of the autocratic sort, so it's a curious term to describe a sales role, but it was dazzling, and people wanted titles.

The more Nutrilite potentates sold, the higher up they would go in the chain and earn perks, such as higher commissions. Get exalted enough and you could set up your own wholesale unit where you didn't just take home the 2 percent kickback from those you recruited, but you'd get a slice of what your recruits earned from their recruits below them.

According to Sam Rehnborg, "The Plan," as Mytinger and Casselberry dubbed it, was "a system bound by personal links and limited only by one's ability to forge them." [14] Now close your eyes and imagine what a drawing of such an organization would look like? Maybe a . . . pyramid? With a shaky, undulating foundation? This never-ending, family-tree-looking web of sellers is a defining feature of all MLMs to this day. Nutrilite just happened to be the first.

In addition to this new compensation model, Casselberry and Mytinger were some wicked pitchmen. Way before Elizabeth Holmes started dressing like Steve Jobs, Nutrilite told their sellers to wear lab coats and carry clipboards if they wanted to nail the doctor vibe. They were encouraged to loiter inside drugstores all over the country, armed with a booklet called "How to Get Well and Stay Well." The booklet contained a long checklist of ailments reps were told to go over with potential customers, including ulcers, headache, constipation, tonsillitis, cuts that healed slowly, anemia, nosebleeds, the common cold, lack of ambition, and "flabby hysterical tendency"—whatever that is. Nutrilite, the reps claimed, could cure all of the above.

The FDA eventually heard about these salesmen dressing up as doctors and shilling a pill developed by a failed sales rep with no medical training. Let's just say the FDA was none too pleased. Though the FDA still hadn't decided exactly what vitamins *were*, it had decided what they weren't, and that was drugs. They were not pharmaceuticals, which under the Food, Drug, and Cosmetic Act had to be rigorously tested before coming to market. Nutrilite was claimed to be as effective—if not more so—than actual drugs, which was a big no-no. So, without the authority to shut the whole operation down, the FDA just seized the egregious pamphlets and sued the company for making false and spurious claims. Nutrilite then reprinted the booklet without the pages that contained the illegal claims, but the FDA seized the booklets *again* because some remaining pages lauded the "discovery" of this so-called cure-all and claimed it was for "those who wanted to get well and stay well." Nutrilite subsequently updated six more pages, but the FDA seized the booklet yet again.

Mytinger and Casselberry fought back against the FDA in court time and time again and claimed the agency was harassing them. Their case went all the way to the Supreme Court, *twice*. The second time, the Supreme Court told M&C to go home and follow the rules.[15]

After four years of litigation, in 1951 the FDA and M&C agreed to an injunction and the Feds handed down the Nutrilite Consent Decree, which basically laid the ground rules for how vitamins and supplements can be marketed to this day. Under the decree, unless manufacturers test a drug through a series of rigorous clinical trials—the standard that allows something to be classified as a drug—they can't claim it "treats" or "cures" anything.[16] Instead they have to use what are called "structure/function" claims that suggest the product can *help* with certain maladies but must stop short of stating it's a cure. Logically, if they can't say it's a cure, they probably don't have proof of its efficacy, and having proof then becomes less of a hindrance to marketing a supplement. This is why today we often see ads for supplements using vague phrases such as "boosts immunity" or "supports digestive health" or "promotes cardiovascular function." Taking calcium does not mean you won't get osteoporosis, but it may "promote bone health." Furthermore, companies can only make statements that have been backed up by scientific research. You can say calcium supports your bones, but you can't say it "promotes clear skin." Finally, if a company wants to add something to their pills that is not essential to human life (such as, I don't know, maybe . . . alfalfa?), they have to put that on the label.[17]

Still, the government remained wary of Nutrilite and other companies that tried to convince Americans to buy products by citing dubious claims about their curative abilities. The same year as the Nutrilite Consent Decree was handed down, the new FDA commissioner, Charles Crawford, boldly stated at his swearing-in ceremony, "We are being plagued with a small army of food quacks peddling nutritional nostrums. America has the most abundant and nutritious food supply and is enjoying the best health of any nation in history. But these food quacks tell us that our foods are of such poor quality that the population generally is suffering from malnutrition. They say that every disease, from cancer and heart failure to irritability and insomnia, is caused by malnutrition. Then they insist that we can't get well and stay well or look younger and live longer unless we supplement our diet with their particular brand of some outlandish food, usually unpalatable, or start dosing ourselves with some simple vitamin and mineral mixture. A vigorous campaign of spreading the truth as well as of law enforcement is needed." Most people would probably have agreed with this anecdotal aggrandizement of the health of the nation, but just a decade earlier, President Roosevelt had assembled a panel of scientists to address what he called Americans' widespread "undernourishment." The consortium published its findings in a paper called "Are We All Fed? A Report on the Diets of Families in the United States," which found that, statistically, Roosevelt was correct in his assessment.[18]

Undeterred

Thanks to the resolution of its beef with the FDA, Nutrilite was allowed to continue operating and continued to grow steadily over the next decade. The company also continued to toe the line between fact and fiction in their marketing materials. In 1958, the company ran an ad in *Life* magazine clearly designed to position the company as a credible, scientific, research-based corporation. The ad stated that Nutrilite had "a sincere desire to make a contribution to the forward movement of all scientific research devoted to the advancement of human nutrition." It described how "part of the research inspired by Carl Rehnborg has involved biological assays through experiments with animals. These experiments have resulted in the conclusion that there are a number of factors which, as yet, have not been isolated or chemically identified. One has been biologically identified in the Nutrilite Concentrate." [19] I can't decide if this is a pitch that would've been written by Don Draper or Peggy Olson.

That gobbledygook and the new business model worked. Between 1951 and 1956, the company's sales increased from roughly $10 million to $26 million, and its share of the national vitamin market went from 6.7 percent to 13.4 percent.

But the Feds were still wary of what Nutrilite was up to and changed tactics to go after what seemed to them like a sketchy deal, top to bottom. This time the Federal Trade Commission took the lead—the FDA and FTC share jurisdiction over marketing supplements—and alleged the company engaged in anticompetitive practices by restricting distributors' ability to sell other companies' products and requiring them to sign a two-year noncompete agreement. The FTC also took issue with Nutrilite's spinning of the new regulations put forth by the Nutrilite Consent Decree as an endorsement of the product by the FDA. Nutrilite even alleged that the court's decision prevented any other supplement company from making the claims Nutrilite did.[20] The FTC ultimately ruled that Nutrilite's two-year noncompete was anticompetitive (I could've told them that), but that the provision in its contracts preventing distributors from selling competitors' products was not.

The distraction brought on by continued legal action eventually led to decreased sales and increased tension between Mytinger & Casselberry and Carl Rehnborg, and in 1958 they parted ways. That same year, two of Nutrilite's top sellers, a couple of best friends named Jay Van Andel and Richard DeVos, left the company to start their own venture, growing it exponentially over the next several years by borrowing the same tiered-commission structure that Mytinger and Casselberry had conceived. In 1972, a year before he died, Rehnborg sold a controlling stake in Nutrilite to this new company, and in 1994, the younger firm bought its predecessor outright. Today, Nutrilite is still around, sold as one of four main product lines for the brand most responsible for the rise and pervasiveness of the modern-day MLM: Amway.

4

The American Way

No company has had more of an impact on the modern MLM industry than Amway, even though it didn't pioneer much in terms of products or a business plan. No, Amway took its sales model directly from the old bosses at Nutrilite and started out by selling quite ordinary household products such as cleansers and detergents. After more than six decades in business, they've grown a multibillion-dollar global brand while simultaneously establishing two of the wealthiest and most powerful family dynasties in modern American history. Acolytes think of Amway as the truest representation of the American Dream in action, a testament to the power of entrepreneurship and a plucky, can-do spirit. Critics call it a pyramid scheme (Scamway is a popular moniker) or, in some cases, a cult.

Today, Amway leads in global annual revenues among all MLMs, at $9 billion, beating out the runner-up, Avon, by about $3 billion. Amway boasts 3 million "independent business owners," or IBOs (Amway-speak for "distributors"), nearly half of whom are in China, and claims that every single day twelve thousand new people join the Amway "family." Amway offers a catalog of around four hundred products— everything from the cleanser they started out with to self-tanning face serum and energy drinks. Amway claims that one in five American households stock at least one Amway item, meaning you probably know an Amway IBO. Do you? I don't, and I've never seen an Amway product in person. Hmm.

But the Amway legacy goes far beyond their profits, which are vast. Betsy DeVos, a major shareholder, and her household alone are worth about $2 billion.[1] What Amway really pioneered was a philosophy—one that has shaped the culture of every MLM that exists today and, in many ways, the idea of what it means to live the American Dream.

I'll let Steve Van Andel, current cochair of the board, former co-CEO, and eldest son of Amway cofounder Jay Van Andel, summarize: "The thread that stitches together freedom and enterprise also, I think, stitched together our entire history."[2] This was part of an inspirational speech he gave to an audience of over thirty-eight hundred top-earning Amway IBOs at a fiftieth anniversary celebration the company held in Las Vegas in 2009. "Nobody can take that idea away. It's why we're all here today. Personal freedom. The freedom to start your own business, to be your own boss. That's what Amway is about."

To understand Amway, you need to understand its founders, Jay Van Andel and Richard "Rich" DeVos, which is pretty easy to do because throughout their lives the two men loved talking about themselves. A lot. Between the two of them they wrote six books before their deaths in 2004 and 2018, respectively. Over time, the myth becomes the story, and the story is part of how Amway continues to recruit twelve thousand people every day.

"The Mate Was a Mighty Sailing Man, the Skipper Brave and Sure"

Before they became some of America's wealthiest men, Jay Van Andel and Richard DeVos grew up in similar humble all-American homes. Born two years apart, both were raised in Grand Rapids, Michigan, the second-largest metropolitan area in the state. Unlike its bigger, more progressive, and notably more diverse counterpart, Detroit, Grand Rapids has, for centuries, been a bastion of American conservatism, rooted in the very Dutch tradition of Calvinism.

Van Andel and DeVos, both of whom came from entirely Dutch lineages, credited their later success and worldview to their Calvinist upbringing. Calvinism, which gets its name from the sixteenth-century Christian reformer John Calvin, is an old-school Protestant denomination that holds among its core values the belief in predestination. Here's how Calvin himself explained the concept: "All are not created on equal terms, but some are preordained to eternal life, others to eternal damnation; and, accordingly, as each has been created for one or other of these ends, we say that he has been predestinated to life or to death."

In case it's not evident, *life*, in this case, means eternal life in the kingdom of heaven, while *death* means eternal damnation in the depths of hell. Before you're even born, God has already determined whether you're going to heaven or hell, and there's not a damn (excuse the pun) thing you can do about it.

So in facing one's terrifying, unknowable, and unchangeable eternity, Calvin's followers sought to find evidence here on Earth that they were on the path to salvation. The idea is that because God is all-knowing, he certainly wouldn't choose lazy, unrepentant sinners or nonbelievers to join him in the kingdom of heaven, right? So, although you could never really know whether you were saved, you were much more likely to be among the chosen few if you had been blessed with the good sense (by God of course) to lead a holy, disciplined life of service. Have you worked hard and been rewarded for your honest work? Do you have a lovely and righteous family? Well, then chances are you're going to the Good Place.

In addition to seeing worldly success as a sign of salvation, Calvinism defines work as a calling from God. These qualities heavily influenced what would come to be known as the Protestant work ethic: hard work, discipline, and purpose are the keys to upward mobility, here on Earth and up there in heaven. To assure *their* eternal spots in the Good Place, the Van Andels and DeVoses lived traditional Midwest middle-class lives marked by discipline, hard work, "family values," and church. According to Jay Van Andel, his mother was a devout believer who ran the household, while his father "repaired and sold cars to provide for his family and bring glory to God."[3] "Two basic distinctives of Reformed churches were the emphasis on the sovereignty of God and the responsibility of man to live faithfully by God's word in every part of life," Van Andel wrote years later. ". . . As I look back I'd have to say that all my political, economic, and entrepreneurial beliefs come from these two tenets of my religious upbringing."[4]

For DeVos, the prosperity part of the gospel was a driving force in his life from the beginning. "I can't dismiss my roots as a kid growing up during the Great Depression in the ordinary Midwestern town of Grand Rapids, Michigan. From the standpoint of money and material possessions, we were barely scraping by," DeVos once said of his childhood. His father was sometimes unemployed and worked at a grocery store and a men's clothing store when DeVos was growing up. He would later quote his dad as saying, "Own your own business, Rich. It's the only way to be free."[5]

Both boys attended the Grand Rapids Christian Academy, and when Jay was fifteen, his dad gave him a car, a privilege few kids at his school could claim. Right away, Jay began charging kids twenty-five cents for a one-way trip to school in his Model A.[6] One day, Rich DeVos, a kid two years his junior, shelled out a quarter for a ride and bingo-bango the two became instant friends. They'd often talk about their dreams of entrepreneurship and promised that they would start a business together one day. "What I wanted—my goal—was to build and succeed in my own business. And I never had any doubt that I could do exactly that," DeVos later recalled.[7]

After graduation, smack-dab in the middle of World War II, Van Andel joined the Army Air Forces, and DeVos followed him two years later. Both held positions on the ground, training airplane and glider pilots, and when they returned home, they decided to use their experience to start their first business: Wolverine Air Service. One of Michigan's nicknames is the Wolverine State, after the ferociously opportunistic animal that used to be abundant there before the fur trade decimated the population.[8]

Anyway, postwar, everyone was jazzed on air travel. "Many people thought every new house would be built near an airstrip and that there would be two airplanes in every garage so we could all commute to work by air," Van Andel said of the "airplane craze" he came home to.[9] So while the idea of two twentysomething high school graduates with no business experience starting an aviation company may seem ambitious, it was nothing if not enterprising. Wolverine Air Service offered chartered flights, a flight school, airplane repair, and airplane sales. Grand Rapids was the furniture capital of America (the home of Steelcase and Herman Miller), so it ended up being a fairly busy hub.[10] Not being pilots, Van Andel and DeVos mostly managed the operation from the ground and found they had spare time to pursue other business opportunities. They opened a drive-in restaurant near the Grand River, a canoe service, and a fishing charter out on Lake Michigan. Van Andel proudly wrote, "Working from nine to five provides an average standard of living; it's the work done from five to midnight that really moves you ahead in life."[11]

In its first year of operation, Wolverine Air Service did quite well. It flew 2 million passenger miles and brought in $50,000. After several more years in business, it had twelve airplanes and fifteen pilots. After three years, Van Andel and DeVos made a decision that feels antithetical to the entrepreneurial spirit they were constantly bragging they possessed. Feeling satisfied in their hard work and earnings, they rewarded themselves with a year off. A whole year! Inspired by a book they'd read called *Caribbean Cruise*, they decided to sail to South America. That was the extent of the plan according to their books: head south. Unfortunately, they had even less experience with boating than they had with flying and purchased a schooner in Connecticut that had been dry-docked for a decade, something any yachtsman would tell you was probably not a great idea for such an ambitious voyage. Unlike cars, which can come out of long storage in mint condition, boats dry out on land and can crack and leak. Van Andel and DeVos made it to Puerto Rico before the boat sank.[12]

DeVos and Van Andel's South American adventure took place during La Violencia, the bloody Colombian civil war in which communist and liberal paramilitary groups fought the military and the conservative government in a ten-year bloodbath that claimed between two hundred thousand and three hundred thousand lives. (Does this remind you of Rehnborg's time in Shanghai or what? What's with these men?) Fleeing the violence on an ocean liner, the two men continued their trip down the west coast of South America all the way around to Argentina, where the dictator Juan Perón was in charge. The two men then took a few months bouncing around most of the other South American countries and Caribbean islands, eventually landing in Cuba, only to call the vacation quits. According to Van Andel, the main lesson they took away from their trip was that socialism is bad and free enterprise is good.[13]

Once back in Grand Rapids, they didn't return to Wolverine

Air Service, but instead took stints as ice cream peddlers, toy salesmen, and door-to-door sellers of baked goods. As disorganized as all of this sounds, they *did* make some money and set up a company in which they invested their profits, called Ja-Ri, after Van Andel and DeVos. Will the bromance ever end? (No.)

Around this time, they also learned that, while they'd been witnessing the scourge of socialism in South America, Van Andel's parents had started using Nutrilite, which had been sold to them by one of Van Andel's cousins. Mom and Dad Van Andel loved the product so much, they convinced their son to talk to that cousin about selling it. At first, it wasn't easy to move Nutrilite, given the newness of the vitamin market. But Van Andel wasn't worried. Referring to the recruitment aspect of Nutrilite's business, Van Andel once said, "The qualms some people have at the thought of selling vitamins quickly disappears when the prospect of making a lot of money enters the picture." After a rocky start, the two attended a sales meeting where they got so pumped up about the business that Ja-Ri soon turned all of its attention to selling Nutrilite.

The product wasn't what moved them; it was the sales model. What the founders of Ja-Ri believed and based their Nutrilite sales model on was mainly decentralization. They preached that a centralized, "normal" corporation, with its leaders and middle management and plebes, gained total control over its business by killing the dreams of the people on the bottom. "What distinguished Nutrilite was the focus on individuals, not groups of employees," Van Andel once said.[14] Of course they often complained that their company, where they were at the top with rungs of distributors under them with new recruits under them, was commonly and unfairly referred to as a pyramid.

They argued that all businesses had that structure if you draw it on a piece of paper, the difference being that in their company the people at the bottom were in complete control of their destinies. "In an ordinary firm, there is a small, well-paid group at the top composed of the chairman, president, vice presidents, and so on. Under these people is a larger group of managers, and under the managers is the largest group of all—the technicians, clerks, computer operators, secretaries, and laborers,"[15] Van Andel said in his company's defense. "There's nothing sinister about the shape."[16] According to Van Andel and DeVos, this was the ultimate American dream: all you needed was a desire to make money and a little bit of money to put down in the beginning. There was no boss to impress, you made the money you wanted to make working as hard as you wanted to work. All that Ja-Ri was providing were the things you *needed* a big company for: research, manufacturing, and supply. Van Andel and DeVos believed that under Nutrilite's pyramid structure, at least those at the bottom could call themselves business owners and enjoy the freedoms that afforded them.

But think about that for a minute. Plenty of things about direct sellers make them far from business owners, and perhaps make them even more powerless than traditional salespeople. Direct sellers don't control inventory or pricing or what products are available when. Nor do they have equity in the company. They don't control corporate marketing or public image. And most of all, there is no moral code by which others selling the same products must abide; the market, it was said, would sort the wheat from the chaff. Additionally, it was becoming known around this time that most people who entered this type of business did poorly. Rather than seeing that as a failure of the product or of the marketing strategy, companies such as Nutrilite put this failure entirely on the seller's supposed lack of motivation. The companies turned a blind eye to there not being a customer base large enough to explain the revenues and to how the bulk of the money coming in was from sign-up fees from new recruits replacing the failed ones.

Then the government started looking into Nutrilite because of its bogus health claims and all hell broke loose at the top of the pyramid. Around this time, to expand the product line, Rehnborg and his wife launched a makeup line, and in response, Mytinger and Casselberry started their own to compete. The attention from the Feds and this sudden infighting between Rehnborg and the marketing folks created holes in their leadership structures that allowed a seriously problematic (for the MLM owners) opportunity for distributors. With no one at the top minding the store, and with the leadership not even sure of what they wanted to sell—vitamins or makeup—folks began breaking the chain of command. Downlines began going rogue and starting new Nutrilite sales teams without alerting their direct uplines. Trust, something that Van Andel and DeVos preached as the linchpin of their Nutrilite operation, one that claimed $85,000 in "group retail sales" in its first year, began to erode.[17]

What Jay and Rich did next was in line with this sort of sneaky disentangling from the official Nutrilite sales structure. Seeing the chaos at Nutrilite, they decided that the best way to preserve *their* team, the Ja-Ri team, was to diversify its product offerings and step away from Nutrilite altogether. They called their team together to pitch the idea that Ja-Ri should begin selling a completely new line of products. All of their members came on board for the new venture, and Nutrilite lost half of its reps in the Midwest.

"Rich and I put a lot of thought into what product line to add. Whatever it was, it had to be something anyone could sell," recalled Van Andel. Although they'd been successful selling vitamins and supplements, it was sometimes difficult to convince people they needed the product, which created extra work and uncertainty. They also saw how the government could throw a wrench in the works, and they wanted as little to do with the government as possible. So they decided to use their sales team to hawk something that did not have to be demonstrated, would not come under FDA scrutiny, and was already a household necessity that would run out and need to be purchased over and over. "A Nutrilite sale required a one-hour presentation to convince the potential customer of their need for dietary supplements," Van Andel explained. "Our new product line had to be something everyone knew they needed."[18] The confidence they had in the business model was seemingly all they needed, with the actual product being an afterthought. "We picked cleaning products," Van Andel said.[19] In particular, they went with a soap that was already on the market called Frisk. They found a manufacturer in Detroit and purchased a 50 percent stake in Frisk, which they renamed Liquid Organic Cleaner, and changed the plant's name to Amway Manufacturing Corporation. Similar to *Ja-Ri*, *Amway* was a portmanteau, of *American way*.

Before selling any soap, they sat down and wrote a more strict sales and marketing plan, or the Plan, as they called it, which created a rigid hierarchy; this is where you start seeing titles such as Silver and Gold and Emerald and Diamond being bestowed on members of the organization. In 1959, they did away with their Nutrilite-associated Ja-Ri moniker and adopted Amway as the name for the entire corporate entity. One of the first exclusive buyers they procured for their cleaning products was Monsanto Chemical. Yes, *that* Monsanto, of Roundup infamy.

Under the Plan, sellers were encouraged to sell to people they knew, rather than knocking on the doors of strangers, who are liable to slam the door back in your face. Each seller purchased product from Amway at the same discount regard-less of rank in the organization. You earned money based on a complicated points system that factored in the amount of sales your downline produced in a month.

The Plan also focused heavily on recruitment, where promises of wealth and freedom were made to potential new-comers. Presented very much as an opportunity to "share the wealth," recruitment came with its own rigid set of directives, laid out in *The Amway Career Manual* given out at "oppor-tunity meetings," weekly gatherings where *successful* distribu-tors gave their pitch to unsuspecting marks.[20] The manual instructed these distributors to "announce to your guests that you would like to tell them about an exciting opportunity to be in business for themselves. Explain that it is an opportu-nity that grows as they share it with others. . . . Would they be interested in a chance to realize their dreams through a busi-ness of their own?"

The recruiters were told to ask their potential recruits a bunch of questions about how they saw their future, suggest-ing new cars or houses were on the horizon. "Ask if they are as successful as they would like to be. If not, would they be in-terested in a chance to realize their dreams through a business of their own that they can build on a part-time basis—and, with such a modest initial expenditure?"[21]

Then, lest anyone get the wrong impression, one was to draw the business model as structured like a flower, not a pyramid. Finally came the promise the recruits could easily make $1,000 a month with Amway.[22]

In 1963, to make extra-sure everyone in the organization wouldn't do what the founders themselves had done in starting the business, Amway published a directive called "The Amway Rules," including the following:

- ▲ **Retail store rule:** No selling Amway products in stores or at fairs or as a fundraiser for your kid's school.
- ▲ **Advertising rule:** Only people high up in the organization could hang a sign or post an ad saying they sold Amway.
- ▲ **Customer protection rule:** Each distributor had an exclusive right to sell to any new customer they gained for thirty days, which sounds like a good thing, but after thirty days any other Amway seller could scoop the person up as a customer. This incentivized rapid recruiting.
- ▲ **Cross-group-selling rule:** One could only sell at wholesale to those below one and buy from those above one. No sideways dealings.
- ▲ **Price fixing:** No seller could earn more by changing retail prices or buying at a discount from the seller's upline. Exceptional profit had to be made in some other way.

But DeVos and Van Andel weren't just selling financial opportunity and soap; they were selling free enterprise. Like many conservatives of the time and today, they believed that self-reliance was synonymous with success. A quote repeated by Van Andel from John Calvin reads, "No work will be so mean and sordid as to not have a splendor and value in the eye of God," which Van Andel interpreted to mean that work for oneself is virtuous and makes God happy. Van Andel qualified the glory of such free enterprise, saying it doesn't pertain to porn or prostitution or being an abortion provider or writing books he deemed dirty. Other than that, though, God loved it. No longer was your self-worth and actual worth left in the hands of those who signed your paycheck, it was predetermined by the Lord and proven by you with His blessing.

The pitch worked all too well. Even though Van Andel and DeVos weren't the first direct sellers on the block and even though they weren't selling exciting new products, they grew fast. Ten years into business, in 1969, the company had eighty thousand active distributors (who knows how many inactive or failed entrepreneurs were left in their wake).[23] In 1972, their ranks numbered three hundred thousand. Compare that to the number of grocery stores in America today, roughly sixty-three thousand,[24] and it's pretty clear that three hundred thousand people weren't getting rich selling soap. No, Amway was simply selling the opportunity to maybe sell soap in a fully saturated market. But the company just kept growing.

Next, to expand their product line, Van Andel and DeVos

began trying to replicate Nutrilite, to create a competitor. Whether they put any real effort in or just claimed this was their focus didn't matter. Under their threat of a complete takeover of Nutrilite's market, Rehnborg sold a controlling stake of his company to Amway, which still sells Nutrilite to this day.

Contrary to what common sense would tell us, the next thing that happened may have helped Amway grow: a recession during the national tumult of the early 1970s.[25] In an echo of the climate of their childhoods, Van Andel and DeVos witnessed staggering unemployment, low wages, and inflation crush the country culturally and economically. With the supposed evidence this crisis handed them, that being part of the "traditional economy" was a fool's errand, the Amway pitch became even more enticing. You can get a job, right now, with no experience, no background check, and just a tiny bit of money down. And you can earn limitless dollars. You never have to worry about the government or big business screwing things up, at least in *your* home, ever again. You are the boss now. This appealed to hippies and squares alike, sticking it to the man. By 1977, there were 360,000 Amway members across the globe.

One distributor said he joined around this time after his salary as a university professor shrank: "Along with other college faculty nationwide, I took drastic salary cuts and considered myself lucky to have a job. I wanted income security. I liked the idea of making money, lots of it, without having to show up for work. . . . I wanted to be plucking the fruit from the money tree, not sitting on the outside of the circle chewing pits while others feasted."[26]

Unsurprisingly, as part of their belief in free enterprise, Van Andel and DeVos also preached the gospel of personal responsibility and positive thinking that was rooted in American conservatism and gaining mainstream popularity. Both founders cited among their personal heroes the author Norman Vincent Peale, a Methodist minister whose book *The Power of Positive Thinking* was published in 1952 and quickly became a perennial bestseller for its thesis that having a positive attitude is the number one factor to success. According to DeVos, Peale was a regular speaker at Nutrilite meetings, and one of the first books DeVos read upon joining the organization was *The Power of Positive Thinking*. Later, Peale would become close friends with DeVos and Van Andel, and DeVos would preach the power of positive thinking in his own writing:

I can. It is a powerful sentence: I can. It is amazing how many people can use that sentence realistically. For the overwhelming majority of people, that sentence can be a true one. It works. People can do what they believe they can do. Apart from the few people in the world who are deluded in a psychotic sense, the gap between what a man thinks he can achieve and what is actually possible to him is very, very small.[27]

In other words, you'd have to be literally insane to think that it's difficult to become a wealthy person.

It's funny to think of this sort of thinking as "new" because it has become so commonplace today. As part of that promise to be your own boss, MLMs have adopted an approach to marketing that, for the untrained eye, may make the companies sound less like retailers of protein shakes or essential oils and more like life coaches, churches, or in some, more extreme, cases, cults. Arbonne, which sells makeup and skin-care products, entices people to join them by promising "A surefire way to flourish is being your own boss, and Arbonne can help you do it!"[28] Young Living, which sells essential oils, declares that you will "become part of something bigger" and that "no matter your goal, we want you to know that it is possible."[29] For LuLaRoe's founder, DeAnne Stidham, her goal in starting the company with her husband, Mark, was not simply to sell funky-patterned leggings and stretchy tops but "to encourage and challenge people to do their best! We wanted them to lift each other up, to become friends, and to cheer each other on!" She goes on to call LuLaRoe not a company or a retail brand, but a "movement."[30]

And then there are the inspirational quotes distributors recycle over and over online. Search Pinterest for "mlm quote ideas" and you'll get thousands of unattributed suggestions such as "No one is cheering harder for me than the girl I used to be" or "You only fail when you stop trying." Hashtags such as #girlboss, #bossbabe, and #fempire punctuate most sellers' recruitment posts, undergirding captions that explain how if they try to recruit you to join them in their "business opportunity . . . it means that the girl boss in ME sees the girl boss in YOU!" [31]

But unlike traditional business owners who take on an enormous amount of risk and, statistics show, have in their first five years a 50 percent chance of failing, MLMs essentially claim that, by joining them, your financial success is *guaranteed*. Assuming you're willing to put in the work, there is absolutely *no reason* why you shouldn't achieve the life of your dreams. The key is staying positive and believing in yourself, no matter what setbacks you face.

This is a lot easier said than done, so many MLMs now offer self-improvement courses and tools to help sellers stay motivated and on track, many of which come with a fee. dōTERRA, for example, offers Empowered You, "a personal development program designed to help you learn, love, and live your strengths every day." The course uses a strengths-assessment tool that's been popularized throughout the business world to help dōTERRA's Wellness Advocates "embrace your strengths because when you do the results are power-ful."[32] Amway offers its distributors nearly one hundred free courses designed to help them grow their businesses, but has loads more instructional material available by subscription.[33]

In addition to company-sponsored seminars, a whole new subindustry of motivational coaches has sprung up in the past several years specifically centered around the MLM community. One coach, Jackie Ulmer, who runs a website called StreetSmartWealth.com, promises, "More Money, More Time, More Freedom, More Peace, More Influence, More Opportunities." Her site lists dozens of affirmations, some of which are categorized by the time of day you should say them to yourself. Before bed, you might try, "As I sleep, I know my mind is being conditioned for more success," while "I am deserving and there is plenty of abundance in the world to go around for everyone" can be deployed any time of day. She also suggests recording yourself uttering these phrases so you can listen to them on the go (as if listening to a recording of yourself would ever be easier than just saying the thing out loud).[34]

The underlying message of all these treacly phrases is much less motivating once you dig a little deeper. Because the flipside of believing you're 100 percent responsible for your success is that, if you fail, you have no one to blame.

This message is especially convenient to deploy when sellers, customers, and other observers begin to question certain

MLM business practices. In April 2017, LuLaRoe cofounder and CEO Mark Stidham used a company call to address complaints from sellers that they'd received wet, moldy inventory that they couldn't sell. "I've heard some whining lately also about 'Well, my inventory's stale,'" he said, after a long monologue comparing selling LuLaRoe clothing to working on a farm. "No, you're stale. Your customers are stale. Get out and find new customers. If you bring a new customer in, then your inventory isn't stale."[35] During what was supposed to be a motivational Instagram video for distributors, DeAnne took aim at distributors who were having a hard time selling. "[Someone] sent me an email that said, 'I'm just so upset because my business can't succeed because I don't have the leggings to take care of all my customers!' Well, guess what? You're obviously in the wrong business." In other words, it's not that we are having supply issues, it's that something is fundamentally wrong with *you*.

This mentality is just about as old as the MLM model itself. In her book *Best Wishes*, Brownie Wise, the original Tupperware lady, offered encouragement to her flock: "Synchronize your thinking, you are the commander of your fate, and the zero hour is now. Success is the blue ribbon of attainment, and failure is the booby prize of life. If you can name it, you can have it. That's the only rule in life's continuing contest, the one entered the day you were born."[36] This quasi-intellectual and spiritual word salad meant to place all responsibility for outcomes on the individual has often proved sufficient to keep failing distributors from bailing, convinced that if they just try a *little* harder and believe in themselves a *little* more, they'll eventually achieve the success they've been promised. When you look at the typical MLM founder, it's easy to see why people would believe this. The industry is full of millionaires who often have few credentials to support their success other than extremely high self-esteem and a penchant for talking a good game. But sometimes they talk a bit *too* loudly and it spells disaster.

5

Mind Games

Rankings. Titles. Discounts. Awards. Pink ·Cadillacs. Winners, losers, and everyone in between. The MLM world is a bizarre land where incentives can range from the opportunity to buy your own ticket to a conference to earning a new rank based solely on products you've purchased that now sit in your garage. The disincentives are just as plain: once you've roped in your friends and family, quitting seems off the table and an admission that you sold them a bill of goods.

Even today, sorting out what is actually part of running a business and what is just a bunch of love bombing or shaming, what part of your business is done out of guilt and obligation, and what actions will actually make you money, is mind-numbingly difficult. We can thank William Penn Patrick for figuring out that this sort of obfuscation and psychological manipulation are great tools in growing an MLM.

William Penn Patrick was born in North Carolina in 1930. Like so many MLM founders, he didn't show a ton of early potential, and it took him a while to figure out what he wanted to do with his life. He quit school at fifteen and took a number of odd jobs—busboy, gas station attendant, and door-to-door utensil salesman—to get by. He then served in the air force during the Korean War. After dropping out of the University of Illinois because it was "too easy," he earned a teaching certificate from Sacramento State College in California. He later served as an elementary school teacher for three years (a job for which, given how the rest of his career would play out, he seems almost criminally ill-suited). Then he quit. "I wanted to get out and get that millions of dollars I was after—and I couldn't do it on a teacher's salary."[1] That he thought this line was worth someone writing down is hilarious.

Then, in the early 1960s, Patrick made a decision that would change the trajectory of his life completely: he became a distributor for Nutri-Bio, an early MLM similar to Nutrilite that sold nutritional supplements and, also like Nutrilite, faced intense scrutiny from and had several of their products seized by the FDA after claiming their supplements could treat everything from the common cold to diabetes.

Nutri-Bio's founder, John Shoaf, was reportedly inspired to start the company after attending a motivational speech on "the laws of success," and just two years later, the company's vice president, Jim Rohn, a former evangelical preacher, was quoted as saying that sales would reach $300 million within five years. "We'll have a product for everybody, from the cradle to the grave," he said. Indeed, the company offered a huge variety of products including supplements for babies, protein shakes, nutritional wafers, and even flavored straws. (Despite his company's promises of miracle cures for all, Shoaf died of pneumonia at age forty-nine.)

Nutri-Bio's greatest legacy was not *what* it sold, but how it sold. A 1962 *Maclean's* article about the company compared its marketing plan to a "get rich quick scheme" and described its training program as one "which takes ordinary people and converts them into high-pressure positive thinkers with the zeal of missionaries out to convert the heathen." The president of the company was known to preach, "People who fail are negative thinkers."[2]

Patrick was here introduced to the MLM ethos: unapologetic hucksterism plus performative enthusiasm plus a penchant for making people who don't strike it rich feel so bad about themselves they'll sink money into the scam against their own interest. Patrick loved the idea so much that he decided to mastermind his own MLM enterprise. According to his authorized biography, by R. C. Allen, Patrick had early on set a goal of becoming a millionaire by age thirty-five. At thirty-three, with no clear path ahead, he began to "develop his marketing plan. . . . Then he looked for a product."

There are two stories about what happened next. In the widely shared version, Patrick was walking down the street in his neighborhood of San Rafael, California, when all of a sudden he noticed an intoxicating scent filling the air.[3] Transfixed by the odor, he began to follow it warm-hot-hotter style until he found himself standing outside a stranger's garage. The door was open, and the garage was filled with boxes, which Patrick figured might be the source of the smell. Looking to investigate, he knocked on the front door. The owner answered and explained that the boxes contained fruit-scented beauty products he'd purchased from a company called Zolene Organic Cosmetics.

Zolene was founded by two women, Zoe Swanagon and Helene Fly, hence the name. They used foods including almonds, avocados, and honey in their concoctions, which they marketed as all-natural and preservative-free. Although they were perhaps ahead of the natural-beauty curve, the lack of preservatives meant mold sometimes grew in their products, but that discovery came later. The year that Patrick discovered the brand, in 1964, Swanagon and Fly were selling their products in health food stores and beauty parlors and, apparently, to wholesale buyers such as the man with the garage.

The homeowner had intended to resell the products for profit but hadn't figured out a way to move such massive inventory. Sensing an opportunity to put the sales skills he'd learned at Nutri-Bio to work, Patrick offered his neighbor $16,500 (roughly $150,000 in today's money) for the entire lot of what sounds to me like Bath & Body Works products.

The other story, told in Patrick's biography, is a lot less sexy but sounds more likely. In looking for a product to fit his sales model, Patrick chose the Zolene cosmetic line on purpose, he sought them out. The small company was operating out of a garage and was struggling to make a profit. Patrick thought that if he combined their product with the right marketing plan, he could save the company and make millions.[4] One of the first things Patrick did after signing a deal with the owners was to rename Zolene. He chose Holiday Magic. Why? It's unclear. To me it brings to mind . . . wait for it . . . the holidays. Such as Christmas. But that's not at all what the packaging or products suggest. Perhaps he was going for more of a British take on *holiday*? He rebranded the products, too, dressing them up with catchy names such as Lemon Face Splash and Papaya Dew Moisture Cream. Because of the obvious fruit smell and the claims Zolene made about the nature of their ingredients, Patrick initially marketed the stuff as "all-natural," but as time went on, he switched suppliers to save money and dropped the claim before the FDA could catch a whiff of anything misleading.

Then he began recruiting. He had a tiny office in San Jose where he'd interview folks to populate the top positions in the company, those directly under him. The official biography dispenses quite rapidly with what happened next: fewer than three pages are spent addressing how Holiday Magic went in less than a year from an idea to a million-dollar company with hundreds of distributors. Several testimonials from that time credit Patrick's spellbinding demeanor and worldview, as he was always there to listen and encourage, righteously so. "I made this decision because I believe in the principles of Bill Patrick," said one recruit. "They center along the same lines as mine." According to Patrick, success all boiled down to doing the right thing: "Right thoughts create right principles and the result you eventually receive is right actions."

He also preached radical honesty as the best way to make money. "Total honesty means you must look at yourself, admit your mistakes, correct them, and never, never make them again." He talked a lot about exceptionalism: "Average means the best of the worst and the worst of the best." He spoke of the haters, and how they are gonna hate: "No matter who you are or what you do, sooner or later someone is bound to criticize you. It is something you must learn to face." He compared himself to Abraham Lincoln in that he would do the right thing, always, even if it meant he might die for his cause. (Patrick didn't have a full understanding of Lincoln's assassination, obviously.) And Patrick said the primary issue with most people who are unsuccessful is a lack of courage. You get it.

With these quippy bites flying all over the place, Patrick also coined new terms for his recruits. The entry-level recruits were called General Distributors, or the Generals. Their goal was to recruit people called Master Distributors, or Masters, to work under them. The Masters would in turn recruit a level beneath *them*, the Organizers. All of these positions required a considerable buy-in from participants, ranging from a few hundred dollars into the thousands depending on where you set your sights. Then, the lowest tier in the sales hierarchy, the foot soldiers, were called Holiday Girls. They could join the company for a relatively modest sign-up fee of $50 and were the only recruits charged with actually selling any product. To do this, they either went door-to-door or hosted parties, typically dressed up in outfits reminiscent of mod flight attendants and carrying magic wands, along with cases of product. A 1967 ad for the opportunity to become a Holiday Girl read:

Holiday Magic has opened a new world of profit and fulfillment to many women just like you. Today over 25,000 of them are Holiday Girls, building exciting careers, adding to their personal and family income. . . . You don't need a college education or business experience to be a Holiday Girl. You *do* need a dream—and the confidence to make it come true.[5]

The ad also claimed that Holiday Girls' sales took the company from a $16,000 profit in 1964 to over $5 million in just three years. In one often-repeated story, Patrick boasted that one of his distributors, late on his rent, offered his landlady a Holiday Girl position in place of payment. After her brief training, she said, "My mother tried to make a lady out of me for twenty-five years. Holiday Magic did it in four days."

Recruitment into the higher ranks often happened at "opportunity meetings," where distributors were instructed to make ridiculous displays of wealth and promise vast sums of riches to anyone who joined the company.[6] These could take place in any old building, but the walls had to be adorned with Holiday Magic banners and ads. Every distributor in attendance was tasked with bringing along five potential recruits. Holiday Magic provided scripts to use in various recruitment scenarios. Such as: "I have discovered a business opportunity that is really great! And there is more money in it than anything I have ever seen and I would like to invite you to come with me and look at a real money tree!"

Another script assumed you knew the target: "Joe, I've discovered something that is really great! There's more money in it than anything I've seen and I'd like to show it to you, too. I think it would fit you like a glove."

It was a simple and enticing prospect: any regular person could become a hugely wealthy success if only that person had the guts to go to one meeting down at the VFW or a church basement. Once there, the General or Master who was hosting gave a speech about the magic that Holiday Magic had brought to *his* life. With the goal of signing everyone up on the spot, the company instructed recruiters to start with a soft sell: "So, will you join us?" If that didn't work, the recruiters should quickly move to an emotional hard sell, as outlined in the official Holiday Magic manual for how to hold these meetings:

> Our objective is to bring our prospect to the point where he feels excited at the end of the meeting, he feels a ray of hope and an inkling that this may be his way out of his financial problems—he can think of only three things: himself, money and Holiday Magic. He likes the way he feels, so his thoughts must be compatible—HIMSELF AND MONEY THROUGH HOLIDAY MAGIC! . . . Our prospects are going to make their decisions to join us because they "feel" right about it in 99 cases out of 100.[7]

Holiday Magic taught specific techniques to help distributors nail the emotional hard sell, a tactic still used by many

MLM salespeople today. First there was the Assumptive Attitude, which urged distributors to assume the person wanted to sign up and that they should act accordingly. Subordinate Questions were seemingly non-sales-related questions (e.g., "Did you have breakfast?") designed to elicit a yes and hopefully get the recruit in the *habit* of saying yes. The Impending Event was Holiday Magic speak for a limited-time offer, a way to convince potential recruits to enroll today or risk losing out on this incredible deal. Cash Money Enrollment was simply code for showing off how much money you had so people would think you were successful and want to get in on the action. For example, recruiters were told to stuff their wallets with bills and open them frequently in front of the recruit to show off how much money they were just carrying around. You could also sew large bills into your coat lining to casually flash them in a jokey fashion. If those comparatively subtle flairs failed, you could always just throw money in the air while shouting things like "HM stands for Hot Money!" I'm not making any of this up.[8]

If all else failed, you should resort to all-out belittling, such as asking your mark to explain multiple times why he doesn't want to make money "until he feels stupid" and signs up. Or you could follow Patrick's own script and imply that anyone who hesitated to join Holiday Magic was a lazy fool by telling them point-blank, "There is no reason why you shouldn't be earning thirty-three hundred dollars a month at least. If you can't do that, then get out."[9]

The training manual also had a whole bizarre section about how to get a pen into someone's hand, and tips for getting people to sign the contract once they did. Recruiters are told to sneak a pen into the target's hand beneath eye level so it feels as if it magically appeared there. They should drop a pen and, when the target picks it up, tell the person to sign the paper with it. If you can get the targets to take the pen, pull out a second pen to use as a pointer, instructing them where their initials are needed. This way they won't try to return the pen to you.

Word Salad Days

The plan worked—to a point. By August 1966, Holiday Magic was reporting $2 million in annual sales.

To Patrick, this was proof that all it took to get ahead in life was a positive attitude and a plan. So he decided to take things to the next level. See if he could *really* make a name for himself. In addition to his goal of becoming a millionaire by thirty-five, a young Patrick had it set in his mind to become a successful politician, ultimately president of the United States.

His platform was based on anti-communist beliefs and a

fervent capitalist bent: "Few people understand the difference between selfishness and greed, so an increasing number of them begin to accept the concept of something for nothing as their rightful heritage. . . . A beggar asks for crumbs, and he deserves what he gets—crumbs. . . . Instead help the beggar to help himself." In speaking about public assistance, his attitude was even gnarlier: "The general concept of welfare is a something-for-nothing concept kept alive by politicians who are afraid of losing favor with the parasites who take unfair advantage of those who work and create our wealth. And there are many such parasites. They give nothing of value to an economy or society, yet they demand to be clothed and fed." Parasites! You can imagine what type of potential constituents he hoped to win over.

His plan was first to be elected governor of California in 1966 (never mind that schmuck Reagan), continue to be rich, get reelected in 1970, and head on over to his new office in the White House in 1972. He announced his gubernatorial campaign in November of 1965, and even though a pollster bet that Patrick would be lucky to earn 1 percent of the vote in the Republican primary, he remained undeterred. He spent around $350,000 of his own money on the campaign, but it wasn't enough; he only nabbed a little under 2 percent of the vote. This was a heavy blow to his worldview that if you just believed something, such as, say, becoming leader of the free world, you could make it happen. Not content to accept defeat at the hands of democracy, Patrick accused that pollster, Mervin Field, of accepting a bribe to slant the polls against Patrick—a claim for which he had no proof. Field sued Patrick for defamation and won a settlement of $300,000.

One skill Patrick did have that seemingly all politicians yearn for is the ability to compose baffling word salads that sound profound but are actually nonsense. Imagine hearing this, an excerpt from a column he wrote in Holiday Magic's 1967 company magazine, on the campaign trail. There are no edits here:

> Growth has its unique problems, both for a company as well as a person. Expansion is habit-forming once inertia is gained. Your whole life must become equally expansive. A parallel need of understanding and greater capacity of mind is essential to keeping your circuits from being shorted. A word of advice from one who has experienced what you are now finding true about growth. Man is best known by the company he keeps and the pleasures he seeks.

Come again? With his political career thwarted, Patrick turned his attention to spreading his gospel of radical self-reliance and individual optimism through a different medium—the burgeoning self-help industry and, in particular, its counterculture stepchild, the Human Potential Movement (HPM).

Psyops for Dummies

You might not know his first name, but you've heard of Abraham Maslow for sure. He's the American psychologist who came up with that pyramid-shaped model of human needs, called Maslow's hierarchy. At the bottom are such things as food and water and sex, and as you move up the pyramid, you get to such needs as safety, love, self-esteem, and finally self-actualization.

In 1962, Maslow published his famous book *Toward a Psychology of Being*, where he presented his theory of self-actualization. He argued that human beings have a fundamental drive to reach their full potential, whatever that means, and that this drive could be facilitated by positive relationships with others, a sense of autonomy, and opportunities for creativity and personal growth. Whereas earlier psychologists such as Freud were more deterministic—what your mom does to you as a kid will set the course for your future—Maslow believed if you work hard enough on yourself, you will achieve a sort of nirvana here on Earth, mother be damned.

We were just about to enter a time of much tumult in American culture—a time when many people felt helpless, what with the Vietnam War draft sending tens of thousands of men to their deaths and protesters at home contending with violence—and Maslow's humanistic psychology became a popular antidote to disillusionment. You can, with the power of your mind and determination, overcome fear and hopelessness. You can, just by deciding to, have a good life free from fear and negative outside influences. Naturally, this idea evolved over the years. Many modern approaches such as mindfulness-based therapies share some of the basic assumptions of humanistic psychology, including the importance of subjective experience, personal growth, and meaning making.

The Human Potential Movement (as it was deemed by *Look* magazine in 1965) was an offshoot of this humanistic psychology that emphasized personal freedom and self-determination, with the underlying assumption that people were inherently good and capable of positive change so long as they put in the work.

This sounds pretty nice compared to that Calvinist stuff, right? Maybe you aren't doomed to hell after all? HPM took these humanistic tenets and added to them the notion that if you could harness that freedom and you were determined enough, you could unleash your potential on the world *and* it would make you successful. Money wasn't the only measure of success in HPM, but since it usually is in the wider culture, the pursuit of wealth became an indication that you were a true devotee.

If this sounds familiar, that's because similar versions had been around long before Patrick was even born. For instance, after the Industrial Revolution and the abolition of slavery shifted labor forces in dramatic ways, Andrew Carnegie—the steel magnate and philosopher, not to be confused with Dale Carnegie (né Carnagey) of *How to Win Friends and Influence People*—published an article called "The Gospel of Wealth."

This original Carnegie helped popularize the bootstrap mentality in the United States. He claimed to be a self-made man, born to a poor family in Scotland, who worked his way up to a position of great power in the American steel industry. What he failed to remind people was that his uncle was a powerful politician, and his uncle's son, George, was one of the main architects of the Industrial Revolution, so it's not exactly the same as you or I becoming a tycoon. Carnegie was approached by that cousin to start the Carnegie Steel Company. But, yeah, otherwise he *totally* bootstrapped it.

Claiming to have met that Carnegie and interviewed him at length (a claim that has never been corroborated and is denied by Carnegie biographers), Napoleon Hill would popularize this aspirational line of thinking in his bestselling book *Think and Grow Rich*.[10] The book, published in 1937, is still so popular that is has almost one hundred thousand reviews on Amazon. From that book to *The 48 Laws of Power* to *The Secret*, Americans are forever obsessed with the power one's mindset has over one's success in life.[11]

William Penn Patrick fully embraced HPM's ideology, creating his own version with the Leadership Dynamics Institute (LDI), which basically taught Human Potential Movement ideas in group therapy, sometimes called encounter-group training. Patrick claimed the LDI, through the practice of radical honesty in front of a group of strangers, would rid you of your hang-ups so you could achieve everything you wanted in life, including all the money. "Wealth comes from giving something of value to other persons who are willing to pay for this value. Each man in a free society is rewarded by his fellows in accordance with his contributions to his fellows. Should you desire wealth, find a better way of giving what you have to offer to more people. The more people you can help, the more people will pay you for this help." That's a quote from LDI's teachings, but again just sounds like a jumble of obvious statements.

LDI was also an MLM and deeply intertwined with Holiday Magic. From 1967, the institute would serve as the elite training program for Holiday Magic distributors who wanted to advance their careers.

For $1,000—nonrefundable—you could spend a weekend learning Leadership Dynamics with higher-ups from Holiday Magic, the unwritten promise being that you'd get to earn a higher commission or a new title if you completed the course. That was a big if; the course was brutal. In 1972, a scathing (and hard to stomach) tell-all book called *The Pit* came out, written by a former Holiday Magic distributor, Gene Church. It exposed Patrick's methods and the truth about LDI.

Church says he first heard about the program not through

his upline in Holiday Magic, but from an ad he saw in the magazine *Specialty Salesman*. Beside a photo of Patrick, the ad proclaimed, "You have to be tough, smart, and ambitious to attend this man's class." Church asked other Holiday Magic sellers who had attended what the experience was like as he was deciding whether to plunk down a grand. To a person, he said, all of them spoke of it as "the greatest experience of their lives." Church signed up to see if he could become the man the advertisement described.

The seminar took place at a Hyatt in Palo Alto. About forty men and women—mostly white, educated, married, and involved in Holiday Magic, gathered on a Friday morning for a welcome breakfast of toast and jam. First, they were asked to sign a contract releasing the LDI leadership from liability in the event of any psychological or physical harm. Everyone signed. Next, they stood at attention as four instructors entered and explained why they were all there.

"'You may have noticed some of the things here in the center of the room. I'd like to take a moment to explain what they are and how we might possibly use them,'" Church recalls one of the hosts saying. "'You see before you a coffin, it's open. Coffins are used to bury people in. It's possible that here in this class we have one, two, or more people who are already dead and just don't know about it yet. If we find someone like that, what we're going to do is put them inside the coffin, and we'll leave them inside there for as long as it takes them to realize how much it means to be alive.'"

Then the instructors introduced a metal cage in similar fashion, along with a cross, which would be used to demonstrate what real persecution felt like, and a noose, which hung there with no explanation at all. The General who was leading the weekend promised the experience would "break through all the lies you live with and teach you to lead better, more truthful lives." He delivered three rules that, without context, must've been terrifying: no hitting in the face with a closed fist, hitting with a closed fist on the body was permissible, and never hit an instructor. So whatever they were doing here, whatever Church had spent $1,000 on, involved physical violence. He didn't run. He stayed, and the attendees split off into a group of twenty-four men and a group of twenty women.

What came next was an experience Church says he couldn't believe was actually happening; sometimes it forced him to question reality. The *pit* referred to the center of a circle of chairs where one by one participants would be subjected to LDI's coursework. Here's a sampling: One obese man was made to strip naked in front of the group, get in the metal cage, and eat as much as he could in one minute from a bag of kitchen trash. Another, also naked, was beat on his buttocks with a Ping-Pong paddle until he began to bleed. The only way he could make it stop, said the instructor, was to admit he'd had an affair and simulate having sex with the woman. Afterward, he turned around to see his wife standing in the corner.[12]

This went on and on with each attendee forced into the pit. The only explanation, Church says, for this bizarre and brutal treatment was given by one of the instructors toward the end of the weekend: "We have to get physical because if we didn't, all you fuckers would lie." The closing lecture was about a pledge of secrecy, that no one in the room should explain to anyone outside the room what had happened.[13]

The Pit was adapted into a fictionalized film called *The Naked Weekend,* and these scenes are the kind you'd watch through your fingers, if you could handle them at all. Some victims eventually filed suit[14] for the abuse, and Patrick, forced to take the stand, showed no remorse about his institute's tactics. When asked if people were nailed to that cross Church described, Patrick said they were merely tied there. The prosecutor pressed on:

Q: "How was one individual tied to the cross?"

A: "Well, how would you normally tie somebody to the cross?"

Patrick was prodded about burying people in coffins and asked if he had considered whether anyone suffered from claustrophobia. He replied that the person would get over it and that the coffin was nice and modern, with a pillow and everything. "You would like it," he told the judge. About the beatings and physical abuse, he said, "I don't think those things are damaging . . . a little painful, but a man learns from his pain."[15] All this coming from a guy who looks a lot like Pat Sajak, the host of *Wheel of Fortune*.

To Infinity and Beyond

Reading Church's and the court's accounts of LDI brings to mind a more recent MLM—NXIVM, the infamous group whose leader was Keith Raniere. Raniere had been involved with Amway in the 1980s before joining another MLM with a similar structure and product offering, Consumers' Buyline Inc. CBI was later shut down after dozens of states filed lawsuits proving it was a pyramid scheme. Undaunted, Raniere then started a vitamin MLM company, National Health Network, but that one went kaput in just a couple of years. During this time, Raniere seemingly fell in love with the MLM business model and began developing an MLM called Human Potential Development. HPD initially sold professional-leadership and personal-enrichment courses, while also selling the opportunity to sell those courses. This organization eventually morphed into NXIVM, which began to market trademarked seminars such as Executive Success Programs.

Since its inception in 1998, NXIVM had enrolled some eighteen thousand people, holding adult summer camps in upstate New York and offering what seemed to be simple personal-development courses and conferences all over the country with Raniere as the vaulted leader.[16] These courses could run between $5,000 and $10,000 according to court records. But then, you know, megalomaniacs gonna megalomaniac, and a decade after it was founded, Raniere turned NXIVM into a cult of personality, and then an actual cult. He created an inner circle of female members who paid extra for the privilege of learning "female empowerment" from a man.

In DOS, or Dominus Obsequious Sororium, which is Latin for "lord over obedient women," members were starved, had sex with Raniere, were forcibly branded with Raniere's initials, blackmailed with pornographic images of themselves Raniere required them to create, and also made to attend midnight volleyball games and retreats in the woods if they weren't locked inside their apartments for disobeying Raniere, or Vanguard, as he rebranded himself.[17] All very culty, but NXIVM was an MLM whose participants were rewarded for recruiting other participants. Notable Raniere quotes include "Humans can be noble. The question is, Will we put forth what is necessary?" and "Knowing what to do is useless without the emotional strength to do what you know."[18] Eventually, in 2017, several former members went to New York State authorities with these allegations and more. Raniere and a handful of the women closest to him in the organization, including *Smallville* actress Allison Mack and Seagram's heiress Clare Bronfman, were charged with racketeering, sex trafficking, identity theft, fraud, extortion, and more! All were found guilty, and Raniere will spend life in prison while the women all pleaded guilty and received sentences ranging from probation to eighty-one months in prison.[19]

The ideas of limitless potential and that anything can be achieved through a combination of optimism and willpower are not unique to MLMs. If anything, they're quintessentially American ideas. But all successful MLMs use some version of this thinking because they have to. Ultimately, hope, not beauty products, nutritional supplements, or weight-loss products, is what they're selling. At the annual dōTERRA convention in 2021, CEO David Stirling delivered a presentation about leaving behind your "limiting beliefs," saying, "dōTERRA has a particular way of helping, and maybe it seems, at times, even forcing people to become something greater. . . . In order to do that, you have to leave behind your limiting thoughts and these perceptions, negative perceptions, behind you."[20] In between filtered photos showcasing their various beauty and wellness products, another MLM called Jeunesse features inspirational quotes on its Instagram page encouraging its 152,000 followers to "stay determined" and "be the game changer" and reminding them that "progress is a process" and "if I want to, I can."[21]

We, and by *we* I mean me and other critics of this kind of thinking, now have a name for it: toxic positivity. An ethos that says upward mobility and happiness are possible if you want it badly enough, and if you can't gain either, you're just being weak and pessimistic. What the power of positive thinking, the Human Potential Movement, and other mindset ideologies ignore is reality. The reality is that no amount of willpower or determination by one individual can overcome a system built on exploiting the masses. I think we can all agree about the existence of one-percenters, yes? That the richest 1 percent of the population possess twice the amount of money that the other 99 percent share.[22] That is simply the status quo in our current capitalist faux meritocracy. But somehow we all maintain hope. Hope is one of the most beautiful but vulnerable qualities each of us possesses, and the folks who sell this mindset ideology know that those who should be hopeless, the disenfranchised and those who lack self-esteem, are actually the most desiring of the loads of bullshit these folks are selling.

6

The Watchmen

Even though several former acolytes complained about the tactics Patrick employed to inspire Holiday Magic distributors, others embraced his approach fullheartedly. In 1967, a true showman named Glenn Turner joined Holiday Magic as a distributor. The self-described "harelipped son of a sharecropper" from South Carolina, Turner was born with a slight speech impediment, but it never kept him from talking. Aside from that, his pre-MLM biography reads like William Penn Patrick's passed through a game of telephone.

As a teen, Turner was bullied a bunch because of his harelip and stayed home from school to avoid his classmates, only making it to the ninth grade. His parents pleaded with him to continue his education—they didn't want him to grow up to become a farmer—and because of his cleft lip they worried about his prospects for gainful employment. After a particularly bad fight with his father, Turner ran away from home and at seventeen joined the air force. (Y'all, seriously, what is it with the air force and these people!) He was quickly discharged for medical reasons, after which he went on unemployment for a bit, saying he was waiting for his "opportunity" to make good money. When the unemployment ran out, Turner bounced around, working a bunch of odd jobs: driving a tractor, selling sewing machines, working at a furniture store. Until one day his opportunity finally came along.[1]

Glenn Turner had returned home, dejected after so many attempts to hit it big. One day he was standing on the street and saw a former classmate drive by in a convertible. Turner asked how the man got it, and the man invited him to a meeting, promising him that he could earn over $10,000 a month. That meeting was a Holiday Magic recruitment seminar. Turner took out a loan the next day and plunked down $2,500 to join the company. He hadn't even seen the products yet.

In short order, he had a few recruits under him and hit the road looking for more. He noticed how many *other* people were selling Holiday Magic, and how hard it was to find new customers. He called the company and was encouraged to attend a class led by William Penn Patrick himself, and there

Turner had his aha moment. No one that day mentioned the product; all people did was talk about recruiting, and the big reveal of the night was that six thousand more people were signing up that month. Glenn saw where the money was coming from: people, not makeup.

Straightaway, Turner borrowed $5,000 from an uncle to start his own MLM, a cosmetics company called Koscot Interplanetary, which is an unbelievable name for a makeup line. *Kos* was a play on *cosmetics* and *interplanetary* had to do with the space center in Florida near where Turner had set up shop.

The company's business model was extremely similar to Holiday Magic's. After investing $10 for a starter kit, a "beauty adviser" could purchase products from her sponsor (who might be a supervisor or a director) at a 40 percent discount and resell them to the public. At the end of the month, she could earn a bonus depending on how much she'd earned in retail sales.

Koscot also offered participants the opportunity either to invest $2,000 in the company or to buy $5,400 worth of products at wholesale from their sponsor to become a retailer and build a downline. You would earn the title *director* and then purchase products from the company at a 65 percent discount—quite a jump—and sell them to anyone at a markup, including people you recruited. This is the most singular part of Koscot's model: the company set "suggested retail prices" but had no rules around this. Anyone with enough cash on hand could join the business and sell Koscot products for whatever price they wanted (assuming they could find any customers).

Like Patrick, Turner encouraged his distributors to use flashy, questionable tactics to convince people to join the organization. He encouraged recruiters to write their phone number on a $100 bill when they met a promising recruit. Or, if you didn't have that big of a bill on you, you could wave a blank check in a person's face. Turner also tried to create a kind of jubilee environment where people would chant "Money!" and jump around wildly, sometimes getting hurt. He also produced a promotional video featuring distributors with their fancy cars, yachts, and beautiful wives.

But the real show was Turner himself, who was known for his flamboyance and ostentation. He flew around the country on a private jet featuring a portrait of himself on the tail along with the words ON THE GO WITH THE UNSTOPPABLE GLENN TURNER. He toured the United States wearing a bright red suit accompanied by two of his salespeople who were dwarfs. Turner lived in a $3.5 million "medieval castle with turrets and a bomb shelter" in Sanford, Florida, according to a June 1973 article in the *New York Times* headlined "Turner Decrees a Xanadu in Florida."[2] During his pitches, he was said to resemble a circus ringmaster. "We're going to build a sign outside Orlando," Turner once said, "and it will be the biggest sign in the free world. It's a picture of me in lights. My tie will be nine feet long. I don't know how big the harelip will be."[3] Even if you were put off by his ego, Turner was undoubtedly compelling; a poor boy made good. He was inspirational, if not exactly aspirational.

On the flip side, Tuner was well regarded as a philanthropist. He described facing all manner of discrimination—in school, as a salesperson, in the air force. He dedicated a lot of time and money to helping the disadvantaged, especially those with physical and mental disabilities. Koscot employed many workers with disabilities at its headquarters, and Turner was on the board of Goodwill Industries, which is known for hiring workers with mental and physical differences. He built group homes around the country for handicapped children. By all accounts, Turner took a lot of pride in this work. It was in line with his Christian values, and this philanthropy set his company apart from many of the other MLMs operating at the time.

His eccentric persona and financial success with Koscot spurred the excitable Turner to come up with many more business ideas, most of which never came to fruition. Emcot would be a fur company, breeding minks for coats *and* mink oil he could use in his Koscot cosmetics. Fashcot would sell "hair fashions," mainly toupees, which Turner wore. Souncot, with a name that would easily float today, was to be his record label. One company, Dare to Be Great, was a hit. It offered a motivational cassette tape series that he promised would, well, give you greatness. The set cost $5,000. For tapes.

On these recordings, his speech lisping due to his harelip, Turner welcomes listeners to their new existence. "Congratulations! You have just decided to change your life. You are now in the process of becoming a new man. William James, the father of American philosophy, said, 'The greatest discovery of my generation is that we have learned we can alter our lives by altering our attitudes of mind.'"

"Worrying Is Like a Rocking Chair, It Gives You Something to Do, but It Gets You Nowhere"

Turner's displays of wealth—the jet, the custom clothing, the jewels he flashed to new recruits—were part of the pitch, but could never be replicated by others in the company. Most people at both Holiday Magic and Koscot made little or lost their investments before quitting. In 1973, the SEC filed a complaint against Holiday Magic, accusing the company of fraud. The SEC's argument was based on simple math. According to the *New York Times*,[4] "The S.E.C. complaint alleged, that if each investor recruited others at the rate the defendants said was necessary to earn the sums promised, every person in the United States would have to be recruited within one year." The suit sought $2.5 million in restitution to be shared among thirty-one thousand Holiday Magic complainants.[5]

Koscot was similarly singled out by the FTC around the same time. In 1972, the FTC sued the company, alleging it was operating an illegal pyramid scheme and engaging in anti-competitive practices. The commission took particular issue with the company's focus on recruitment as well as its exaggerated earnings claims, which, they argued, could only ever be achieved through aggressive recruitment, not through sale of the products, and was therefore mathematically impossible for the vast majority of participants to attain.

Against Koscot—where the company claimed a distributor's annual product sales could range from $50,000 to more than $200,000—the FTC found, "The Koscot program was organized and operated in such a manner that the realization of profit by any participant was predicated upon the exploitation of others, most of whom had virtually no chance of receiving a return on their investment and all of whom had been induced to participate by inherent misrepresentations as to potential earnings."[6] The findings from the SEC's and FTC's investigations into Holiday Magic were even more specific: while the promised estimate at those "opportunity meetings" for annual earnings hovered around $100,000, the average distributor took home less than $100 per year—and these distributors were likely in the hole if they'd attended Leadership Dynamics.

The FTC also took issue with Koscot's unique distribution scheme. Per the complaint, until early 1969, the only method used by Koscot to distribute its products was by direct factory shipment to distributors, who would sell to the recruits under them. But beginning in March 1969, Koscot required distributors to establish local cooperative warehouses in which their inventories were stored. Such co-ops would provide immediate product availability locally by holding a larger inventory than would have been available to a distributor waiting for something in the mail.

To establish these co-ops, existing distributors were told to relocate the inventory they already had to the warehouse, while new distributors were credited at the co-op with the amount of product due to them. Distributors were required to maintain a minimum inventory at the co-op. By June 1970, 350 satellite warehouses were in operation.

Seeing that money was still coming in and knowing how much product was sitting in these facilities, Koscot stopped filling orders. Turner no longer felt it necessary to have any actual products in the warehouses at all; the company could just *tell* people the stuff was there. But it took a long time for anyone to find out because selling makeup wasn't really the company's business anyway. At the time of the lawsuits, Koscot had fewer finished goods on hand than the number for which it had already been paid by its distributors.

The final judgment against Koscot Interplanetary came in 1975, and Turner lost. The FTC's administrative law judge wrote in the decision, "Aside from the mathematical fallacy inherent in the Koscot plan, an endless chain scheme must, in any event, ultimately fail to provide returns to all participants." Essentially, the judge ruled, Koscot's eyes were bigger than its stomach. With the incentivized recruitment, people as a whole in the scheme could not expect to recoup the money they put in. Koscot was shuttered for good. This decision helped solidify the definition of pyramid selling, which, for a time, described companies where distributors were compensated primarily through recruitment bonuses and sign-up fees as opposed to sales of actual product to an end consumer outside the organization. That's no longer the definition, as you'll soon see.

Glenn Turner would continue with his motivational program Dare to Be Great, and in 1987 he'd be sentenced to seven years in jail for operating the company as a . . . you guessed it . . . illegal pyramid scheme.[7] Some people never learn. Especially once they're dead, which is how William Penn Patrick avoided a similar fate. Just two weeks before the SEC came knocking with papers, Patrick accidentally crashed his vintage World War II fighter plane in northern California, killing himself and a business associate instantly.

This flurry of scrutiny in the early seventies—and success

in so many suits—by federal agencies should have signaled the death of MLMs, but it didn't, because of what happened next.

While the government was taking down Koscot and Holiday Magic, Amway's founders were cozying up to the Republican Party in D.C. Their conservatism naturally led them to align themselves with the party's agenda, which called for small government, deregulation, and a belief in market forces—supply and demand—so strong that no company or government should come between an ambitious man and his money. Amway used their vast resources to further that agenda through political donations as well as relentless advocacy on behalf of policies they deemed essential to preserving the independent, Christian spirit of America. They even created something called the Institute for Free Enterprise, which, among other capitalist rah-rah initiatives, taught basic economics to schoolchildren around the country.[8]

Then, as luck would have it, in 1973, another Grand Rapids native, Gerald Ford, was appointed vice president after Spiro Agnew resigned. The following year, in the wake of the Watergate scandal and Nixon's resignation, Gerald Ford became president. Gerald knew the Amway founders.

Around this time, the FTC began to take a closer look at Amway's Plan, which was eerily similar to William Penn

Patrick's and Glenn Turner's sales approach, and in March of 1975 the FTC filed a complaint against Amway. All the FTC had to do was look at the Plan to find misdeeds: price fixing, for one, is inarguably illegal *and* the opposite of how the free market DeVos and Van Andel lauded should work. The agency also took issue with those wild income claims and found evidence that bringing in $1,000 a month from Amway would be an anomaly as up to 99 percent of participants *lost* money. To resolve these accusations, all Amway would have to do was pinkie swear not to make those same mistakes in the future, but the FTC saw something more egregious in Amway's business plan: it saw an illegal pyramid scheme, and if it could prove that Amway operated as one, the government could shut the company down for good.

The FTC tried the same arguments it successfully used in the Holiday Magic and Koscot cases: a pyramid scheme is any organization that promises large profits based primarily on recruitment (and getting those recruits to stock up on product) rather than a need for the product in the open marketplace. Another feature common to pyramid schemes is market saturation. Recruits are lured in by the promise of big money made by recruiting more recruits. But Amway had been around for a while and had hundreds of thousands of sellers all over the world, and most of them were recruited by people they knew. Large earnings aren't possible if there's no one left to sell to. The only way, at that time, to prove market saturation was by knocking on doors, and that took time. Years in this case.

So, in the meantime, while the government gathered its evidence, DeVos and Van Andel set their sights on nurturing a relationship with the very government that was going after them. In 1975, they arranged a meeting with President Ford that lasted almost an hour and came out of it triumphant. In an interview a month after that meeting, Van Andel bragged that Ford was now well aware of Amway's troubles.[9]

The duo also began boosting conservative ballot initiatives, including Proposal E, a Michigan law sponsored by a group called Taxpayers United. Amway gave the organization $30,000 for a measure that would cap taxes and government spending in the state at 8.3 percent of its GDP.[10] The long and short of the argument around spending caps: they limit how much money the government can spend, with the hope of lowering taxes and providing more private funding of social services. The measure passed in 1978 with 52 percent of the vote.[11]

The next year, perhaps emboldened by the political power they'd successfully wielded in Michigan, Jay Van Andel became the chairman of the U.S. Chamber of Commerce, which—and this may come as a surprise—is not actually a government body. The Chamber of Commerce is, to this day, as it's now run by Jay's son, America's largest lobbying organization. Although they kind of come across as an organization for the people, perhaps a consumer-protection lobby, or something like the Better Business Bureau, the Chamber of Commerce actually represents business interests, not customers. They lobby for free trade agreements, tax incentives for corporations, and fewer regulations on businesses. You get it.

Immediately, Van Andel began calling for the United States to cut back on corporate regulation and to create a constitutional amendment to balance the budget. "The American economy, we believe, is in trouble, because our government has too long operated in a fiscally reckless fashion—ignoring basic economic principles in favor of short-term political goals," he opined on the Senate floor. The amendment passed in the Senate and was sent to the House, where it died. Still, Amway was now officially operating, in a sense, inside the government. The calls were coming from the basement!

One week after Van Andel's appearance in Congress, on May 9, 1979, the FTC issued its ruling. It said Amway's Plan had "the capacity to deceive" recruits by dangling the carrot of financial freedom. As predicted, Amway said sorry and promised to knock it off, officially revealing that the average monthly earnings were closer to $67, not the promised $1,000. But the FTC commissioners stopped short of declaring Amway a pyramid scheme. The company continued on.

It was a stunning loss for the FTC lawyers who had argued the case in front of the commission. The lawyers believed they had a slam-dunk case. They employed the exact same arguments they had used to win the Holiday Magic and Koscot cases, and the commission had agreed with them. So, what happened here? Well, Amway took that pinkie swear just a little further this time and claimed that the company had *another* set of rules already in place to ensure that it wasn't operating illegally. No one has found evidence that these "rules" existed ahead of their being presented before the commission, but the commission bought it regardless and stated that Amway wasn't a pyramid scheme because:

1. Distributors were required to buy back any merchandise someone in their downline no longer wanted.
2. Distributors were required to sell 70 percent of their inventory (at wholesale or retail) each month to qualify for bonuses.
3. Distributors were required to make at least one sale to at least ten different retail customers each month.

See? We have a rule that there must be real customers and that no one gets left holding the bag, and we won't go so far as to say 70 percent of inventory must be sold *outside* the organization to earn a bonus (thus allowing distributors to earn bonuses on goods sold to their downlines), but we promise we're good boys.

This ruling was a blessing for Amway and a curse for the

public, who now had fewer defenses against predatory multi-level marketing schemes. Jay Van Andel, in his autobiography, credits the FTC investigation for the company's continued growth: "Not only did it teach us something about dealing with the government and bureaucracies, it gave us renewed credibility that we could use later on. If someone questioned the legitimacy of the Amway Plan, we could say, 'Look, the FTC had the same concerns you do. They investigated us thoroughly and we came out okay. We're even used as a model of the right way to run a direct-selling business.'" How often do people have to question the legality of your business for you to come up with a standard comeback? *Hmm.*

Using what have since been referred to as the Amway Rules, countless MLMs can argue that they, too, aren't pyramid schemes because they operate just like Amway and Amway got the government's stamp of approval. One thing to note about these rules, though: How would you know if they're being broken? The FTC is just asked to *believe* that this is what Amway tells downlines and directors and that everyone is sticking to them.

Cut to today, where LuLaRoe, for example, is using a version of the Amway Rules to argue its way out of countless lawsuits. LuLaRoe, which manufactures stretchy leggings, shirts, and dresses in bold and often objectively hideous prints, first made a mistake in requiring sellers to inven-

tory load, that is, to have a lot of clothing on hand to sell in
Facebook live events or at craft fairs or parties. At first, there
seemed to be a real market for these fashions, but with the
help of social media and the greed of the founders, the company suddenly had so many new recruits it couldn't fulfill
the orders it was requiring them to make. The quality of the
merchandise went down. So, rather than say, "Hey, we need
to slow down here so we can catch up," LuLaRoe instituted
a new buyback policy. So many sellers took advantage of this
to off-load piles of damaged or flimsy items that the policy
was almost immediately revoked. The founders accused sellers of abusing the system. Thousands of sellers are still sitting
on inventory with no market and no refunds. All because
Amway won in 1979.

"While the Commission did bring some pyramid cases,
they involved extended litigation, a confusing legal standard,
and a requirement that it prove that the 'Amway rules' were
not enforced," wrote former consumer litigator Bruce A.
Craig in a letter to the FTC. "The unfortunate by-product of
this litigation was the implication that other companies, such
as Amway, were legal since they were not sued. The Commission has never revisited the Amway decision to see if in fact
it does have retail sales and a meaningful buy-back program."

Craig goes on, "The 1979 ruling made billionaires of the
Amway founders and funded a highly effective public rela-
tions and lobbying effort which, for the past 30 years, has

entrenched the dubious principles of the Amway decision and influenced a significant number of legislators and other governmental officials both state and federal."

In 1979, the same year they beat the FTC, DeVos and Van Andel were listed among *Fortune's* top four wealthiest Americans, with an estimated worth of $300 to $500 million each.[12] At the time of this writing their families have a combined net worth of over $10 billion.[13]

7

From Prophets
to Profiteers

In the spring of 2020, amid the backdrop of panic surrounding the emerging coronavirus pandemic, casual users of social media may have noticed a new type of post appearing in their feeds:

> This is to inform us all that the pH for corona virus varies from 5.5 to 8.5. . . . All we need to do, to beat coronavirus, we need to take more of an alkaline foods that are above the above pH level of the Virus. Some of which are: Lemon . . . Lime . . . Tangerine . . . Orange . . . #covid

The above is from a real post shared by a distributor for dōTERRA, an extremely popular MLM based in Utah that produces and markets essential oils and proprietary essential oil blends for use in homeopathic remedies and aromatherapy.[1] This is purely anecdotal, but chances are if you've seen an MLM product on store shelves or at an earth mother's house, it's from dōTERRA. Despite its being against company policy to sell its products at traditional retail outlets, you'll find their oil collections at health spas, crystal shops, and alternative-medicine clinics, adding an air of legitimacy to the brand. But make no mistake, dōTERRA is an MLM.

Although dōTERRA got its start marketing its oils simply as more "pure" than its competitors', over the past few years distributors have begun making increasingly bold, often downright bogus, claims about their health benefits. The government has taken notice.

Given the difficulty the Amway decision created, the Feds in recent years have gone after MLMs less for being pyramid schemes and more for making false claims. During the Ebola outbreak of 2014, the FTC issued dōTERRA a warning after complaints rolled in that certain distributors were advertising that dōTERRA oils could combat the disease (even though, it should be noted, there is still currently no approved cure for it). "Oregano is effective in inactivating MNV (non-enveloped murine norovirus) within 1 hour of exposure," wrote one dōTERRA distributor on social media. "Some of the primary uses for oregano include athlete's foot, candida, canker sores, Ebola virus, intestinal parasites, MRSA, ringworm, staph infection, viral infections, warts, and whooping cough."[2]

It might be soothing to think an oil derived from plants you can grow in any home herb garden could cure serious disease, but the suggestion is potentially deadly. Not only might it lead patients to avoid legitimate and successful treatments for the false hope found in a bottle of oily perfume, but the oils can *cause* serious harm to the body. Over the past twenty years poison control centers across the country have seen a steep rise in calls regarding essential oils. In Tennessee, the number doubled between 2011 and 2016, and most calls were regarding poisonings in children. In 2018, the state of Georgia received a record-breaking one thousand calls involving essential oils.[3] Not only can they cause skin irritation, but if ingested, as a lot of essential oil companies recommend, many popular oils, including eucalyptus, tea tree, camphor, thyme, and wintergreen, are toxic to humans. The list of what could happen to you or your child if you drink them is long and includes vomiting, respiratory failure, cerebral swelling, seizures, and even coma. But that hasn't stopped essential oil makers and their purveyors from continuing to loudly preach the benefits of oils as a part of a healthy diet. DōTERRA has even gone so far as to offer empty capsules, like the ones pharmacists use, made of "inert vegetable ingredients," as part of its product line so users can ingest the oil in pill form. The only warning dōTERRA issues? "If using with essential oils, it is not recommended to pre-fill capsules for future use as the properties of the essential oils will compromise the vegetable capsule."[4]

The government is well aware of the danger of this sort of marketing, which is why the FTC sent a letter to dōTERRA early on during the COVID pandemic, in April 2020, telling the company to knock it off. "It is unlawful under the FTC Act, 15 U.S.C. § 41 *et seq.*, to advertise that a product can prevent, treat, or cure human disease unless you possess competent and reliable scientific evidence . . . substantiating that the claims are true at the time they are made," the letter read.[5] The letter went on to tell the company to stop making such claims, to tell their distributors to stop making such claims, and to email the agency's COVID-19 task force "describing the specific actions you have taken to address the FTC's concerns."[6]

DōTERRA was hardly alone in needing a legal refresher. The FTC sent out hundreds of letters to companies— MLMs and otherwise—that tried to profit on the fears of COVID-19 by claiming their products offered some magical defense against or cure for the virus. "In the fight against COVID-19—Keep moving every day and eating healthy!" read an ad from a distributor of Isagenix International, an MLM that sells weight loss products such as protein bars and shakes. "Isagenix shakes boost your immunity 500%!"

"#VIRUS_CORONA Worried?" read a social media post

from a distributor for Plexus Worldwide, another MLM that sells nutritional supplements. "I've been boosting my immune system for several years with high-quality Plexus supplements. You can too! #Plexus provides excellent all-natural supplements that truly work. Be sensible—not fearful." Have no fear, Plexus Worldwide is here!

The FTC letters all ended with the directive to immediately stop publishing such claims—either directly or via distributors—and to respond within forty-eight hours letting the agency know the companies had done so.

Step Right Up

MLMs present a unique challenge to regulation for authorities. While the FTC has the *authority* to go after companies engaging in deceptive marketing—such as saying cinnamon oil can cure diabetes—in practice, the FTC has little *power*. Ensuring that individual companies do what they're told requires a lot of resources, and as we saw in the discussion of Carl Rehnborg and Nutrilite, the law still provides a lot of gray area as to what makes a health claim illegal.

Before 1906, when the first national legislation appeared around food and drug safety, sellers were not prohibited from making false therapeutic claims on packaging and in sales pitches, and they didn't have to provide proof of what was in any food or drugs they marketed. One could just bottle up . . . whatever, pitch it to the public, and make some cash. Capitalism was being tested in its purest, newest form: the market would decide if something was a good product. Spurred on by industrialization, the gold rush, a transcontinental railroad, and a slew of diseases no one could cure because penicillin hadn't yet been discovered, snake-oil salesmen flourished across America.

Historians still debate the origins of the term *snake oil*, but the most-agreed-upon story is that when Chinese laborers came to America to help build that transcontinental railroad, they brought with them some remedies to soothe their aching bodies after endless days of brutal labor. One of those remedies was said to come from water snakes, and if you rubbed it on your joints, you'd feel better.[7] Come to find out, the omega-3 fatty acids in actual snake oil, like those in fish oil, have been found in some studies to rival NSAIDs such as aspirin and ibuprofen in their anti-inflammatory effects. So there was something to this treatment, but since no one knew what it was and water snakes weren't available everywhere, other versions started popping up that contained God knows what. And hucksters started selling those across the country.

The most famous of these salesmen was Clark Stanley,[8] and his backstory won't surprise you at this point. Born in 1854 in Texas, he grew up to become a ranch hand but decided he'd rather be rich and took a short educational trip to a Hopi village to learn natural medicine, or so he said. He began concocting his own "snake oils" and wrote a forty-one-page handbook about them, and about himself and about being a cowboy. He used the book at sales presentations to look smart and accomplished. I mean, how many people can claim to be authors? (LOL @ me.) He was definitely skilled at one thing, though: ripping people off. Dressed in a fancy suit and christening himself the Rattle-Snake King, Stanley began touring the country chopping heads off rattlesnakes in front of huge crowds while preaching the benefits of his Snake Oil Liniment,[9] which he said could cure, among dozens of other things, neuralgia, lame back, toothache, sprains, frostbite, bruises, sore throats, and snake bites. He got so good at this he was given a stage at the 1893 World's Columbian Exposition in Chicago. The bottles sold for about fifty cents apiece, which is close to $14 in 2021 money. About in line with the cheaper essential oils you can get today.

In 1917, eleven years after Congress created the Food and Drug Act to protect consumers from people like Stanley, his tinctures were found to contain no snake oil whatsoever, just mineral oil, beef fat, and turpentine, along with some culinary spices such as capsaicin, which is found in hot peppers. Gross. His business was shuttered for good and he was fined $20,[10] or the equivalent of the cost of forty bottles of his Snake Oil Liniment. From there, *snake oil* became a catchall term for any vitamin, supplement, or medicine making unsubstantiated claims. The next year would see an explosion of businesses like Stanley's thanks to a disaster closely resembling the pandemic we face today: the 1918 influenza outbreak.[11]

Newspapers and magazines were chock-full of advertisements for cure-alls or preventive tinctures that promised to eradicate the Spanish flu. It was caused by a novel H1N1 virus that was thought to come from birds, though similar to the ongoing debate around coronavirus, that hasn't been definitively confirmed. It's said that one-third of the world's population became infected over two years with over 50 million deaths. Everyone wanted to find a cure or preventive concoction. There was a beef gravy (yes, beef gravy) that boasted it "increases nutrition and maintains vitality in the system, and thus an effective resistance is established against the attacks of the influenza organism." People bought it, literally. In Wisconsin,[12] a doctor was known for administering camphor oil intravenously to desperate patients. Considering that the most common legitimate pharmaceutical prescriptions you could get included heroin, cocaine, and opium, it's easy to see how other scary-sounding treatments could enter the mainstream. Though the government did crack down, in fits and starts, on the sale of these supplements, the industry continued to thrive.

The great danger today is that those messages of alternative cures can spread much faster thanks to social media, and thanks to the massive modern wellness industry. Spurred by dissatisfaction with and earned distrust of the traditional medical community and Big Pharma, wellness culture has risen, made popular by celebrities such as Gwyneth Paltrow and her brand, Goop; by a whole host of social media influencers; as well as by companies such as dōTERRA that capitalize on our desire to feel better and look better "naturally." The industry is estimated to be worth over $4 trillion today, with no signs of slowing.

The 2020 Netflix docuseries *(Un)well* explores the rise of this industry and the impact it's had on our health and our wallets. The first episode is entirely dedicated to essential oils, and dōTERRA is a main character. In the episode, one Diamond-ranked dōTERRA rep, Allison Huish, pitches new recruits by telling them a harrowing story about how she was diagnosed with a brain tumor at age twelve. She underwent surgery, but then her tumor couldn't be treated with chemo, and the idea of radiation sounded "scary," she says. To her credit, it is. But Huish was so scared that when a friend of the family recommended treating her cancer with frankincense and clove oils, which they said had "anticancer properties," her family began administering the oils daily. She also took oregano and tea tree oil to fight bacteria and viruses, she says, but her family made sure never to tell her doctors about this self-medicating. "My mom was very careful that she never brought up that we were using essential oils," Huish explains to a roomful of potential recruits. "If she had told my neurosurgeon that, he could've easily called Child Protective Services." (Hot tip: if you're aware you're doing something to your child that would get CPS involved, stop doing it.)

Huish concludes the story, "And ever since then, I've used essential oils." On-screen we can see that she is alive, so confirmation bias kicks in and one might think, "Wow, yes, the oils worked." Immediately after her pitch, some of the women begin asking how to treat *other* ailments, such as diabetes, with dōTERRA. "Essential oils help clean up the blood . . . but we're not supposed to say that essential oils cured this disease. That is due to the FDA. Our health care system doesn't really like essential oils. It takes away from our Big Pharma and all of those sales."

That's some slippery and skillful language, with Huish basically saying what she can't be saying lest she get in trouble with law enforcement. The spiel about our health care system not really "liking" essential oils is a cornerstone of many MLM supplement pitches these days. *The government doesn't want you to have this, so you can't buy it at the drugstore. You can only get it from me, your friendly neighborhood oregano-oil dealer.*

One huge hole in this logic: If the oils worked, wouldn't this evil Big Pharma create a monopoly on them and mark them up and get richer? Never mind that, antiestablishment thinking often only goes as far as declaring the powers that be evildoers; there's no burden to explain how or why they'd want to deceive the masses. Just think of the idea of the illuminati. Why do they exist? To be in charge. Of people and money. And scene.

Huish was right about one thing: the government doesn't want people to say that essential oils are miracle cures. But it's not because they compete with Big Pharma. Quite the contrary. While there is some, albeit inconclusive, research that shows certain oils can help improve mood or relieve stress, there is absolutely no evidence that they have any role in combating illness or disease.[13]

Unfortunately, the very selling structure of MLMs, though legitimized by the 1979 Amway case, still makes it easy, if not imperative, for bad or just clueless actors to act illegally. That's not to say that individual sellers intend to hurt their customers; these sellers often believe their hype, but harm is harm either way. Think of all the blood diamonds you have lying around.

In 2018, the FTC published "Business Guidance Concerning Multi-Level Marketing,"[14] a kind of cheat sheet about what *not* to do if you want to stay out of the regulator's crosshairs. Item 15 provides a perfect example of how much the FTC can actually do and how nonthreatening their threats can be. It begins, "The FTC has long supported industry self-regulation as an efficient way to secure consumer benefits and promote a robust and competitive marketplace. MLM self-regulation may create these same types of benefits." The

FTC is saying that it doesn't want to get in the way of a free market, it's not trying to hinder business in any way, but it does place a lot of trust in these companies and it is watching to make sure that trust isn't violated. The FTC goes on to say as much: "Belonging to a self-regulatory organization, however, does not shield MLMs engaged in unfair and deceptive practices from FTC law enforcement action. Under appropriate circumstances, the FTC can and will bring law enforcement actions against companies that claim to follow self-regulatory guidelines but in practice do not. Similarly, the FTC can and will bring law enforcement actions against companies that, despite following such guidelines, nonetheless violate the FTC Act." In other words, we're trusting you to follow the rules and if you don't, you'll be in trouble. And if you pretend you didn't know you were breaking the rules, that's on you, not us.

So, we trust you, but we don't *have* to trust you. And besides, who can stop independent distributors from saying whatever they want on their private social media accounts? They are the owners of their own small businesses, after all. A letter to the president of a company surely can't make its way all the way down to each new recruit. And remember, MLMs place responsibility for failure—or illegal activity—on the distributors, not the company or its products. Any CEO of an MLM can throw their hands up and say, "Well, we can't control what independent distributors say. Besides, right here on our website it says that's a no-no." The Amway Rules paved the way for this passing of the buck and made it standard practice.

This has been the case ever since Carl Rehnborg and Nutrilite encouraged distributors to dress up as doctors and plant themselves in local pharmacies with that broad health checklist to present to customers. No one at Nutrilite said you *had* to do this to sell their vitamins, but if you wanted to succeed? That's up to you. Carl knew he was onto something but didn't live to see the day alternative therapies would so publicly, and successfully, compete with mainstream medicine. The wellness arm of the MLM industry offers a unique case study into what can happen when an MLM run by people without medical degrees gets into the business of selling so-called healing products. One of those people can be credited with creating both of the top essential oil companies in the world.

The MLM that started it all was called Young Living, founded in 1993 by Gary Young and his then wife, Mary. According to company lore, Young had become a devout practitioner of essential oils after a logging accident in his early twenties left him unable to walk. After two failed suicide attempts, Young tried a "cure" of drinking water and lemon juice exclusively for (reportedly) the better half of a year. (This is now known as the Master Cleanse and is not recommended for more than ten days.)[15] Young claimed the liquid diet got him up and moving again, and he decided to devote his life to providing relief to others both physically and financially. There's no evidence anywhere to back up this story.

In 1981, the then thirty-two-year-old opened a natural health clinic outside Spokane, Washington. With only a high school education, and a few uncompleted classes in naturopathy, he opened Golden Six Health World,[16] a facility that offered a variety of alternative-medicine services, including some that he himself developed, such as taking blood samples from patients "to interpret them"—meaning examine them for signs of trouble. How Theranos-y. He said he could detect cancer cells and had developed a holistic regimen to cure the disease.

One of the services offered at the clinic was a blood analysis for pregnant women, to see if they were getting the vitamins and minerals they needed, and its popularity led him to offer these clients water births at the clinic.[17] On September 4, 1982, Young attempted to deliver his own daughter, but he and Mary—who also had no medical training—kept her underwater for more than an hour. The child died, and the Washington State Department of Licensing and local police staged an undercover sting operation of the facility, which landed Young in the local jail for the night,[18] charged with practicing medicine without a license, which was only a misdemeanor if you can believe it.[19]

Later, Young moved to Tijuana and opened another clinic,

where he developed a blood crystallization test and something he called "orthomolecular cell therapy," both of which he claimed could be used to treat or cure most of the world's ailments. He promised cancer patients that after a $6,000, three-week stay in his clinic, their cancer would be in remission, but for $10,000 they could be completely cured, forever.

Word spread through Southern California about this miracle worker just south of the border. Tijuana is still a popular destination for Southern Californians looking for medical procedures cheaper than those in Los Angeles or San Diego. Cheaper and more experimental. After hearing about a number of Angelenos who had sought treatment at his clinic, in 1987 a *Los Angeles Times* reporter decided to send Young a blood sample, except, tee-hee, it was cat blood. Young diagnosed aggressive cancer.[20] The reporter followed up with chicken blood, in which Young found signs of an inflamed liver. The fake doctor wrote, "It appears as though you've recently undergone a high level of upset in your life, which has weakened your immune response considerably. We recommend a supervised program of cleansing, detox and rebuilding." Again, this was the recommended course of action *for a chicken*, but Young didn't know that.

Young's interest in essential oils developed after he met a French lavender distiller at a new-age and alternative-medicine conference in the early nineties.[21] Young traveled to France to learn distillation techniques, and in 1993, after returning to the States, he and his wife founded Young Living essential oils.

Essential oils were gaining popularity, and enough competitors were out there to inspire his unique niche-marketing pitch: essential oils, but make it Mormon. The pitch worked, and today there are over 2 million distributors of Young Living oils in the United States.[22] In 2020, the company claimed $2.2 billion in revenues.[23]

To this day, after his untimely ironic death by stroke at age sixty-eight in 2018, the health guru's company publishes a massive handbook extolling its oils as essential to one's health. It outlines, in great detail, how the "frequencies" of specific oils can alter the "frequency" of the human body, bringing it to equilibrium where everything from anorexia to diabetes to cancer cannot thrive. The book also details the extremely intensive and confusing distillation process using a hodgepodge of quasi-scientific-sounding jargon to help explain why Young Living oils are so pure, and why anything less than a pure, unadulterated oil could pose significant danger to one's health.

The index for *personal use* includes entries on everything from yeast infections to strep throat to strokes, uterine cancer and West Nile virus, as well as autism, multiple sclerosis, and AIDS. One thing stands out about the book above all: the overwhelming majority of footnotes cite the Bible. It drives me nuts! Members of my family sell, but more important and scary, they use Young Living oils to treat all kinds of ailments. After reading the handbook pretty much front to back, I want to scream my concerns at them. Oil cannot cure Lyme disease, even if there's a quote in the Bible written two thousand years before Lyme disease was even discovered. Infuriating! This book is doing too much.

Like those claims made in that five-pound, 640-page, spiral-bound text, Young himself was a bit extra. In videos his company posts on YouTube, he stands before crowds preaching the gospel of Jesus alongside the gospel of essential oils, reminiscent of a televangelist, though more overtly capitalistic. Before his death in 2018, he was planning to build an amusement park featuring a monument with his face carved in stone. He operated clinics in South America where it was said that "patients" could receive gallbladder surgery or intravenous essential oil treatments from the man himself, by the hand of God. As he grew hardened in this approach, some in the company became disillusioned and irritated by Young's bombast.

One of those most over it was David Stirling, then COO of Young Living. He left in 2008 and took with him some of the company's top brass, the director of scientific education and support, the senior director of new market development, a regional business director, and the director of events. Together, they launched dōTERRA. Gutted, Young Living eventually filed a lawsuit against them in 2013, claiming they falsely advertised their oils as "100% pure" when they contained man-made materials. A shit-slinging back-and-forth lasted for years with each side attacking the veracity of the other's marketing materials and claiming disparagement.[24]

But then Gary Young kicked the bucket and the contentious relationship cooled amid booming success for both companies. While Young Living remains a godly enterprise, dōTERRA markets itself as much more mainstream, advising customers to add a few drops of lemon oil to homemade cleaning products or to put lavender oil in a diffuser to help aid sleep and reduce stress. Other than that, the two companies' product lines are virtually the same, and both are wildly successful. Although you can purchase essential oils at the grocery store or on the internet, the two MLMs are by far the biggest companies in the industry, with more than a billion dollars in annual sales each.[25] Given the selling structures of the companies, it's impossible to know how many of those dollars are profits or are made from retail sales to people outside the organizations.

Too Big to Fail?

The FTC is trying to stay on top of the money. Even though the Amway case made it legal for companies to use the multi-level recruitment structure, it did uphold the idea that it was illegal to make false promises to people about how much they could earn selling soap—or any other product—and the FTC continually targets MLMs for doing this. In 2020, in addition to the letters it sent to various MLMs for claiming their products could treat COVID-19, the agency targeted a dozen MLMs (including dōTERRA and seven other MLMs that were also sent letters about health claims) that used the economic devastation caused by the pandemic to their advantage. Apparently direct sellers all over the world read headlines about millions of people being laid off or given reduced pay, and they saw dollar signs. One dōTERRA seller wrote:

Need to make extra money? Find it difficult to pay your bills? Were you laid off/#fired? Be your own Boss w/doTERRA essential oils. Msg me to achieve financial independence #laidoff #unemployed #cantpaymybills #cantpaymyrent #student #sales #sidehustle #makemoney #stayathomemom.[26]

You may be wondering if MLMs get shut down these days, especially after the Amway decision made the task so much harder, and the answer is yes. Not often, but yes.

In 2019, the FTC settled a suit with AdvoCare, which sounds like a health insurance company but actually sells nutritional supplements such as energy drinks, fiber, and a probiotic called FastMelt, which I assume is referring to melting fat? The company had previously been accused of selling products that contained banned substances, so it was on the FTC's radar already. This time the FTC alleged,[27] "AdvoCare operated an illegal pyramid scheme that pushed distributors to focus on recruiting new distributors rather than retail sales to customers. The compensation structure also incentivized distributors to purchase large quantities of AdvoCare products to participate in the business and to recruit a downline of other participants with the same incentives. The clear directive of this structure was, as one AdvoCare distributor explained during the company's Success School training, to 'recruit business builders who recruit business builders who recruit business builders . . .'"

To even get into Success School, folks were first charged $59 to become a distributor, which gave them a license to sell AdvoCare products *and* purchase stuff for themselves at a discount. To rise in the ranks, however, and make real money, people needed to become "advisors." The only requirement for that was to move at least $1,200 in products each year. The easiest way to get there? Sign others up and encourage them to buy product to start their business. The company had no regulatory mechanism to ensure that these products were being purchased or used by anyone outside the pyramid.

The FTC alleged that the income of AdvoCare advisors was based on their success at recruiting, with the highest rewards going to those who recruited the most advisors and generated the most purchase volume from their downline.

AdvoCare couldn't prove otherwise and was ordered to not only pay a $150 million settlement, but the CEO and two top distributors were banned from the MLM industry. The company persisted and has since changed to a single-level direct-selling model, which is a fancy name for modern door-to-door sales. Many companies now call this "direct to consumer"; think Casper mattresses and Birchbox and other stuff you order online and it comes right to your house.

Then, in October 2019 the FTC successfully stopped a company called Nerium from selling a coffee-bean derivative called eicosanoyl-5-hydroxytryptamide as a cure for brain damage and Alzheimer's and Parkinson's disease.

In July of 2016, one of the largest and most established MLMs in the world, Herbalife, faced fraud charges from the FTC spurred on by the efforts of an activist investor named Bill Ackman.

In 2012, billionaire hedge-fund manager Bill Ackman made headlines when he announced that his firm, Pershing Square Capital Management, had taken a $1 billion short position on the nutritional supplement company Herbalife. A short position is basically a bet that a company's shares will decrease in value, and when they do, you get a payout. Shorting a stock is one of the most controversial moves investors can make on Wall Street because of how easy it is to manipulate the market. All you need to do is cause the company to fail.

Ackman went on a crusade, alleging that Herbalife was a pyramid scheme and claiming its products were overpriced and of poor quality. His announcement sparked a public feud with Herbalife and its CEO, Michael Johnson, who vehemently denied the allegations and accused Ackman of trying to manipulate Herbalife's stock price for his own gain. Which he was definitely doing and never denied!

The battle between Ackman and Herbalife went on for several years, with Ackman making a series of public presentations and media appearances to promote his short position and call for regulatory scrutiny of the company. He called on Herbalife sellers to lodge complaints with the FTC, which they did in great numbers.

The FTC followed up on the complaints and in 2016 filed suit against the company, stating, "Analysis of Defendants' [Herbalife's] own Distributor purchase data shows that, even under favorable assumptions about Distributors' market reach and sales price, the overwhelming majority of Herbalife

Distributors who pursue the business opportunity make little or no money from retail sales. Under these assumptions, and assuming no costs other than an individual's total payments to Herbalife, half of Distributors whom the Defendants designate as 'Sales Leaders' average less than $5 per month in net profit from retail alone, and half of these Distributors lose money."[28]

Then there were the clubs. In the years leading up to the suit, thousands of sellers began opening private "health clubs" where members had to pay a monthly minimum for the chance to purchase Herbalife products. According to the FTC filing, "One top Distributor explained in a PowerPoint presentation: [Nutrition Club] Operators need to realize that the end goal is not how many $4.00 services they sell each day as that is not the way for them to achieve their financial goals. Rather, it's upgrading a Consumer to become a Customer and eventually a Distributor and ultimately having Distributors become Operators who will duplicate the Nutrition Club method." To echo that point, the Feds submitted evidence from one member of the leadership circle (another nonsense name for people who have significant downlines in Herbalife), Susan Peterson, who stated at a 2009 Herbalife event, "It's wonderful that we have everybody consuming and we have everybody doing the different methods of retail . . . but you got to think about it, guys, the name of the game here is royalty . . . and you don't get paid royalty off of customers. You get paid royalties off of distributors that you help to become successful to become supervisors."

In its response to the FTC, Herbalife claimed to have actively discouraged such retail operations. "Defendants' rules prohibit signs that state or suggest that Herbalife products are available for retail purchase on the premises. Club owners are not permitted to post signs indicating whether the club is open or closed, and the interior of the club must not be visible to persons outside. . . . In 2012, Defendants estimated that there were 3,700 commercial Nutrition Clubs in the North America region (consisting primarily of the United States); Defendants also claimed that Nutrition Clubs were driving 30–35 percent of the overall volume of product purchased in the United States." Huh.

The FTC eventually stopped short of calling Herbalife a pyramid scheme, but acknowledged that little of its sales were being made to real retail consumers. In addition to the $200 million fine to repay distributors, Herbalife was ordered to restructure its business to a single-level direct-selling model and ensure that at least 80 percent of its sales were made to legitimate end consumers. Its current net worth is around $1 billion, down from $8 billion during peak years.[29] After five years of battle, Ackman eventually dumped his shares in Herbalife in 2017 at a loss.

The FTC then issued a statement warning other MLMs

about how they should behave going forward: "They should ensure that income representations are not false or misleading and that compensation structures do not incentivize recruitment and wholesale purchases unrelated to retail demand. Put simply, the structure of a multi-level marketing business should present a viable retail opportunity." All signs point to no. So why do we keep falling for it?

8

Women's Work Redux

Let me tell you about one of my elementary school classmates. We'll call her Becky, not her real name. But there were a lot of Beckys where I grew up, so if you're reading this, Beckys, no matter how similar the story seems to yours, I promise this is not about any of you.

Becky and I met in the third grade back in the mideighties, and she was hilarious. That's the main thing I remember of our friendship; her quick wit always making me laugh with some lip-synch routine. It was her idea that I have a Madonna-themed slumber party one year; everyone had to wear a side ponytail and draw on a fake mole, and honestly, Becky came the closest to nailing not just the look but the *vibe*. Becky, even by third grade, was just a little bit naughty. She got to have perms and wear trendy clothes and dangly earrings, whereas my mom made my clothes or I wore hand-me-downs and didn't get a perm until I was thirty-seven. She even got to go to a tanning salon. When I moved away in fifth grade to a farm that was in the next school district over—an even smaller one—we stayed in touch and got together on special occasions, but that faded over the years as I moved farther and farther away from home.

Then one day about fifteen years ago, she reappeared in my "life" when, you guessed it, we found each other on Facebook. I was delighted to see that she was in a serious relationship with the sister of another childhood friend of ours, a sister who had been a cool little tomboy with a skater haircut that, according to Facebook, hadn't changed much in twenty years. Now, you can learn only so much about someone via social media, but you can also learn *so* much about someone via social media! I just lurked, never reaching out other than to comment, "Hi! You both look so cute!," under an album of vacation photos or something. Then the algorithm buried Becky's profile for a few years, until one day I got a message that read something like "Hey girlie! Wanna try out some awesome mascara? It's the best I've ever used and I'm running a sale right now! Xoxo," and then some emojis, probably. I didn't respond. This was well before I started researching MLMs, but I'd already caught on that they were not something I wanted to be a part of after getting so many of these messages from so many hometown friends. Maybe I should've written her back, but I couldn't say yes, didn't want to make her feel bad, and didn't trust myself to not try and "enlighten" her. I'm the worst.

I did, however, click the link to the makeup line. Called Younique, it is an MLM, and it was founded in 2012 by siblings Derek Maxfield and Melanie Huscroft.[1] They've recently rebranded, and these days their website repeats some version of "We're here to empower and connect women of all ages, colors, cultures and creeds" on every page, but when I looked at it back then, it practically screamed, *"Makeup for Jesus!"* The owners were Mormon and in the early days used that to connect with potential recruits.[2] Christ was at the center of their pitch and purpose and products, which naturally made me curious about what was going on with Becky. Was she *that* Christian? How had I never noticed? So I went back to her profile, and sure enough, Jesus was there and her girlfriend was not. I clocked these details, closed the page, and filed them away in my memory bank's "Huh, whaddya know" files.

When I started reporting on MLMs, Becky was one of the first people who came to mind. Here was the perfect interview subject: she had *a story* to tell about her journey toward MLMs, I was sure of it. So I went back to her Facebook, confirmed that she was still a seller, and went to send her a message. That's when I found a cache of unanswered DMs from her pitching me products and a business opportunity. I don't know how Facebook hides that stuff and not the *other* stuff (creeps and jerks), but it somehow did. As embarrassed as I was to reach out after accidentally ghosting her for, oh, about six years, I wrote to her and asked her if she wanted to talk about her experience with Younique for a podcast I was making. Then I messaged her again. Then once more. She never wrote me back, understandably.

But through her I realized just how Christian MLMs can be, way back in 2012. Ignorant me would come to find out that the Lord was centered in almost every MLM I'd heard of at that point: Amway, Young Living (which my aunt sold), Mary Kay (which my aunt and my best friend's mom and everyone else in the world sold), and Thirty-One Gifts (which another former classmate sold).

Thirty-One Gifts makes bags, mostly, and one popular model is a huge tote that looks more like a cooler and is popular among the Costco set—youngish moms who haul loads of Gatorade and trail mix to away games in their minivans. You know, the ones with BOY MOM bumper stickers? You know whom I'm talking about. The name Thirty-One Gifts is a reference to Proverbs 31, which is a story in the Bible about a king whose mother has some very specific advice about selecting a mate.

So there's this guy called King Lemuel, and no one is quite

sure who he was or where he ruled because the story in the Bible isn't about him, it's about his mom. King Lemuel's mommy loved him and thought of herself as the authority on what makes a good wife, and in Proverbs 31 she goes on and on about what kind of lady he should look for. She's supposed to be good, duh, but mostly she's supposed to work her ass off. She should be the world's first #girlboss. King Lemuel's mom says stuff like:

- ▲ She seeketh wool, and flax, and worketh willingly with her hands.
- ▲ She riseth also while it is yet night, and giveth meat to her household, and a portion to her maidens.
- ▲ She considereth a field, and buyeth it: with the fruit of her hands she planteth a vineyard.
- ▲ She maketh fine linen, and selleth it; and delivereth girdles unto the merchant.

So she's supposed to be a weaver and a farmer and a manager and peddler *and* a mom and a wife. Exhausting! But perhaps that's the point? Now, I'm no biblical scholar, but what I glean from the text is that wives and mothers must take care of the home and have a million side hustles so their husbands can be seen as successful. Take one look at the oodles of #girlboss coffee mugs or daily journals or Instagram posts and you'll see the same message repeated.

Grind

WHILE THEY SLEEP

Learn

WHILE THEY PARTY

Live

LIKE THEY DREAM

I saw that one on a wine tumbler at T.J. Maxx.

LuLa-No

We've recently had the displeasure of watching one such religious MLM horrifically impact thousands of lives, without apology: LuLaRoe.

LuLaRoe was founded the same year as Younique, 2012, by the couple DeAnne and Mark Stidham. Right out of the gate it was a hugely popular clothing line that offered "buttery soft" stretchy leggings and dresses and skirts and tops in okay-ish prints and inclusive sizes. Though the couple started the company where they lived in Corona, California, DeAnne was raised Mormon in Utah and decided early on that she would use her connections to that community to market these new fashions, especially on social media. The looks were initially described as "modest" clothing, a chaste way of dressing popular among Mormon women.[3]

DeAnne is, like many Real Housewives of Salt Lake City, Mormon royalty. Her great-great-grandfather Hyrum Smith was Joseph Smith's brother,[4] and like the Smith brothers, she has created her own personal folklore. DeAnne says she started LuLaRoe at her home with her daughters, just making maxi skirts for them and their friends, and suddenly everyone who saw one wanted one and a #fempire was born. She started hauling her hand-sewn clothing to flea markets and parties, and before long her husband became CEO, and she, as president, became the official face of LuLaRoe.

At the height of their "success," that face was on social media constantly. That face was on advertisements and on-stage at LuLaRoe events and in pictures with countless fans, er, I mean LuLaRoe distributors. That face was modeling the latest LuLaRoe designs on Facebook Live, which was *the* place for live video content before Instagram and TikTok took over. DeAnne streamed inspirational chatter while driving one of her luxury vehicles. Reporters at *Business Insider*[5] have been following the stench of DeAnne's opulence for years, since right around the time of the company's shocking growth, which began in 2015. They published a revelatory story about her sixtieth birthday party, which was celebrated in 2019 while the company was in the middle of many lawsuits. The theme was a masquerade ball, and some even posed with masks of a caricature of DeAnne's face. From afar, distributors who couldn't make it in person dressed in red and posted adoring photos and videos to Instagram wishing their great leader a happy birthday. The birthday was a lavish affair.

Lavish describes a lot of things about DeAnne. Here's what she looks like: Dolly Parton on a budget. She's constantly dolled up, with tons of makeup and dangly earrings and statement necklaces and cocktail rings. Dresses and kimonos and scarves and stacked heels. She has the kind of blown-out bleach-blond hair that Miss Piggy wears, and DeAnne can be just as charming. She also has multiple homes and a ranch and a private plane. Her husband is just as materialistic. He likes to brag on social media about owning a Koenigsegg, one of the world's most expensive cars, which start at about $2 million. Her flock wasn't appalled by this showiness probably because Mormonism often exalts prosperity, seeing it as a sign of the Lord's blessing to those who follow his word.[6] But it's also important to note that in the Book of Mormon wealth is used as a test: one will receive riches if one lives by the words therein, but people should only do good with their money and not hoard material things. That's a test that the Stidhams, according to the lawsuits and the partygoers at least, failed to pass.

They got popular fast, and for a few years everyone wanted to wear LuLaRoe and sell it. But! In the early days you had to shell out thousands of dollars—like $5,000 to *$10,000*[7] to get started as a retailer, and you had to take whatever inventory they sent you. A very, very expensive mystery box! But women—mostly those same women who need huge bags to take hockey gear to and from their kids' high schools—loved the clothes and the idea of making money off them. In 2015, just a couple years after the company's launch, there were a thousand distributors. Two years later, that had bloomed to eighty thousand retailers. The company had a hard time keeping up with demand (without sacrificing their own wealth), and Mark and DeAnne found cheaper manufacturers and graphic designers, young folks who were forced to pump out hundreds of new prints a day.[8]

Additionally, LuLaRoe purchased so much inventory to keep up with demand that it didn't have anywhere to put it, so they left tons of it sitting outside their warehouse, in the rain and sun, then still shipped it to sellers, who received moldy, unsalable clothes. The market was saturated, in more ways than one.[9]

The Stidhams didn't take responsibility for the decline in the quality or the mustiness of their inventory. They did institute a 100 percent refund policy for a hot second after a scathing report came out in *Business Insider*. Dissatisfied sellers were posting photos online of leggings that tore like "wet toilet paper," specifically on a Facebook forum called Lulafail. But as requests for refunds flooded the company, it rescinded the policy, and many retailers are still waiting, years later, for checks that should be in the tens of thousands of dollars.[10] So a bunch of distributors ended up bankrupt at worst and stuck with guest rooms full of shitty knitwear at best. Lawsuits ensued, including one by the state of Washington accusing the Stidhams of running a pyramid scheme. LuLaRoe settled that one for $4.75 million. Their manufacturer also sued them for $49 million in unpaid bills. And a $1 billion class-action lawsuit brought by sellers claimed that LuLaRoe reps encouraged participants to sell breast milk and take out loans to stay involved in the company.[11]

As in the Amway case, finding proof of wrongdoing in an MLM requires a ton of legwork and a ton of people who are willing to self-identify as both victims and victimizers of their nearest and dearest, so they aren't super common. A few lawyers specialize in these suits, but it's not become a big enough enterprise (yet!) to warrant television commercials calling for participants. Fifty lawsuits have been filed against LuLaRoe, and as of this writing the ones that have not been resolved are in various stages: arbitration, settlement, and so forth. Given the tons of bad press, including high-profile documentaries, that the company is still operating is in no small part thanks to its charismatic leader: DeAnne.

It's fun to just sit and ogle DeAnne, especially after her greed and audacity have been put on display. There's real schadenfreude in seeing this megalomaniac crash and burn, but I've always wondered, How did she get that way? How did a little Mormon girl end up essentially stealing from those she promises to empower, all while telling them they're just not working hard enough to see the money they've been promised? How does a person move about the world with such faux guilelessness harm thousands without seeming to care? In 1969, when DeAnne was just ten years old, her mother and father wrote a book called *The Secret Power of Femininity*.

Maurine and Elbert Startup (for real, *Startup*) had been married for thirty-six years when they published this book and had eleven children, the youngest among them a set of twins, DeAnne and Dianne. Per the book's foreword, written by a friend of theirs who was a plastic surgeon, "Elbert is a polished and dignified gentleman and has held many leading positions of authority in his work, church and community," while Maurine is "a cupid who delights in helping young people in love." [12] The foreword sings her praises as someone uniquely qualified to write this book as "she is one of the women in this United States who doesn't need a frenzied national movement to be 'liberated.'" A year prior to this publication, in 1968, the *New York Times* ran a story titled "The Second Feminist Wave: What Do These Women Want?" [13] Activists from the National Organization of Women explained to the press that they wanted equality and to abolish laws that "keep women at home and in the bottom of the job market but exclude them from jobs that utilize intelligence in any way." Signs at a protest that year included one that read WOMEN CAN THINK AS WELL AS TYPE. If the Startups had got their way, women might not even be doing that.

The Startups met while studying at Brigham Young University, then moved to Pasadena, California, where they catered weddings and founded the American Family and Femininity Institute in 1944 or 1945, depending on which page of their shoddily edited book you're looking at. What did AFFI do exactly? For one thing, they charged women $300 for a thirty-six-hour course called Femininity Forum.[14] Essentially, these were group lectures in how to land a man. They also befriended Phyllis Schlafly, a fierce opponent of feminism, who campaigned against women's rights and the Equal Rights Amendment.[15] (The ERA, which would give women equality under the law, is still not ratified into the Constitution.) And AFFI published the book *The Secret Power of Femininity: The Art of Attracting, Winning, and Keeping the Right Man for You, for Unmarried, Ex-married, and Married Women.* Are you ready to learn that art?

On the title page, it reads, "So You Want to Be Loved. Perhaps You Want to Be Married. Maybe You'd Like to Work with Men without Feeling Competitive." That's the actual punctuation. The gist of the introduction is that women are goddesses and supernatural beings (their words, not mine)[16] who should not be competing with men by becoming all human and whatnot. They do say you can try to do a man's job if you want to, but "please remain beautiful, romantic, mysterious, half-real, half-imaginary delights as soon as you come back home or when we take you out to dinner . . . before it's too late."[17] Too late for what? They don't say.

There's a ton of advice on how to act coquettish. "There is no better school for learning how to be attractively naughty than watching the antics of little children, especially little girls."[18] In nearly every interview DeAnne gives, you will see her trying her best to heed her parents' advice, to be demure and be coquettish, which, as an over-the-hill woman myself, is a near impossibility and makes me feel embarrassed when I try to seem less aged, less experienced, and more childlike. My mother calls it "mutton trying to look like lamb," and now that'll be lodged in your head, too. In the videotaped deposition DeAnne gave for that lawsuit Washington State brought against LuLaRoe, she repeatedly demurs, saying that she has little insight into the business side of the company, can't make sense of the documents she's handed, and any wrongdoing must be the fault of the sellers. "I do not know" is the refrain out of her red-lipsticked mouth as she smacks an everlasting piece of bubble gum.[19]

The book also talks a lot about why men are attracted to much-younger women, and all of it has to do with arousing manliness. How do you become more childlike if you're a "competent, hard-headed, defiant, domineering"[20] woman? Well, try making yourself "the pet of your father, your grandfather, your uncle or your big brother."[21] Or your husband, and then let him be the CEO of your company. Don't forget to "pout pretendingly."[22] Yikes. It strikes me as odd that such a religious family would condone all this pretending, or simply lying, in the name of love.

Mary Kay insiders have told me of similar advice they've gotten from their mentors and uplines within that company. In an unofficial policy called "the husband unawareness plan," you pay a fee to become a Mary Kay lady using various forms of payment and hope that your husband doesn't notice the small checks and credit card charges. (Pro tip: get your own bank account and credit cards.)[23] If your husband *does* find out, the advice is to own up to it, play dumb, or claim you used the money to buy makeup so you could look prettier for him.

You might be wondering if there's any career advice in *The Secret Power of Femininity* that a young DeAnne may have gotten her hands on before launching a massive international corporation that at its peak was worth over $1 billion?[24] No, not much to speak of, outside of the suggestion that one should attain an office job of some sort to be in closer proximity to possible suitors. But! Much is written about how to increase the size of your dating pool; how to come in contact more often with more people who may introduce you to someone you can entice. These sections read as eerily similar to the advice given to MLMers looking for more recruits:

> Learning to become a good hostess is one of the best and quickest ways to increase your popularity with all the young people in your acquaintance. It is also the very best way to enlarge your circle of friends who can introduce you to other men and in that way the snowball grows. . . . You will find it well worth your while to devote your time and attention to acquiring the sincere and devoted friendship of such choice guests. Do thinking for them and win their friendship. Study them and become a choice guest yourself, whom others will want to invite to their parties. As a successful hostess, and as an aid to other hostesses, you will find many more opportunities to attract attention to yourself.[25]

Don't Blame Jesus

For many armchair experts and accomplished reporters, the connection between MLMs and God is one of the reasons that Utah is the MLM capital of the world. Utah has more MLMs per capita than any other state. Certainly, the religiosity of the LuLaRoe founders and other Christian MLMs helps justify in the minds of participants why a company might not be "a bad MLM," but that's only if you think there is such a thing as *a good one.* Without too much generalization here, it's often noted that Mormons and other Christians are especially ripe for the MLM pitch for a number of reasons. Many religious groups don't encourage mothers to work outside the home, many religious groups do encourage their members to support one another's business endeavors, and many religious groups proselytize, which is great training for recruiting in an MLM. So, while without willing victims scams couldn't exist, something grander is happening here.[26] It all comes down to politics, just like every other sketchy thing in this country.

Codified into state law in 1983, Utah's Pyramid Scheme Act[27] stated that creating a pyramid scheme was a felony and participating in one a misdemeanor. A company was a pyramid scheme when "a person gives consideration to another person in exchange for compensation or the right to receive compensation which is derived *primarily* from the introduction of other persons into the sales device or plan rather than from the sale of goods, services, or other property." As you know by now, that distinction is rather difficult to make since the buyer and the seller are so often one and the same. But the law stood for a few decades.

Then in 2005, the Direct Selling Association—the MLM lobby—worked to introduce a bill to amend the state's Pyramid Scheme Act and got it passed. The new law, which was billed as an anti-pyramid-scheme law, actually made prosecuting schemes harder.[28] It stated that if a good or service is purchased by anyone in the scheme, then it's a legitimate business and free from prosecution. State Attorney General Mark Shurtleff testified in favor of the law during hearings. Indeed, during his tenure from 2001 to 2013, Shurtleff cozied up to the MLM industry publicly and unapologetically. Between 1999 and 2012, 14 percent of his nonparty campaign donations (amounting to $475,000) came from the Direct Selling Association. Two years before his testimony, he spoke at an event for Usana, a Utah-based MLM that sells supplements and skin-care products. "If you work hard, you can realize the dream of financial wealth and success," he told distributors. Sean Reyes, who assumed the Attorney General seat in 2013, also has extensive ties to the industry. Reyes, like Shurtleff, received campaign donations from Usana, and in 2017 Reyes spoke at the annual Direct Selling Edge Conference, where he was introduced as "a supporter of the direct selling industry for many years."

On many counts, it does not seem surprising that Utah is known as the fraud state. On the state attorney general's website an article asks if that's true and the first sentence says, "Yes, we are."[29] Backdoor wheeling and dealing has disincentivized the law from going after pyramid and Ponzi schemes alike. In 1984, the *Washington Post* reported[30] on a Utah State fraud task force that found "members of the Church of Jesus

Christ of Latter-day Saints are particularly susceptible to various schemes because faith in one another spawns promoters to take advantage of 'the Mormon Connection.' " But what's been set up in Utah is a big-time scammers' dreamland smack-dab in the middle of a highly trusting religious community. But, sure, it's easier to say, "Mormon women love MLMs."

9

Fool Me Twice

In 1993, Scott Johnson was working a good job at a nuclear power plant in a suburb of Houston, Texas, when a co-worker told him about this amazing opportunity to earn extra cash. Scott was bringing in roughly $60,000 a year working nine to five and raising kids in the suburbs with his wife, so it's not as if he were hurting. But this sounded like a chance to not just live the middle-class ideal, but to blow the top off it, creating explosive wealth the *easy* way. The American way.

"I was approached by a guy that I worked with," Scott recalls. "He was like a midlevel manager at the plant and I was a supervisor, and he was telling me his brother-in-law, who was a medical doctor, is his sponsor and that he practices with a second doctor, who sponsored the first doctor. Then the second doctor was a flight surgeon in the air force, and his sponsor was a Continental Airlines pilot." Scott says that in hindsight he can see that the coworker was trying to get out in front of any suspicions Scott might have about the legitimacy of the opportunity.

After explaining that not only were all the smartest guys the coworker knew in on this, they were all making more money than you could imagine. Intrigued, Scott agreed to meet up after hours at this guy's home, where he promised to give Scott a lot more information about how all of this was possible. The hang was—you guessed it—an Amway pitch.

"After about an hour of a presentation . . . my gut reaction was *I can do that*," Scott says.

His coworker was keen enough to warn him that if Scott told people he was selling Amway, they might think he was in an illegal pyramid scheme. Remember, the 1979 Amway case got a lot of national attention and wasn't that long ago. "But we're not your father's Amway; we don't go door-to-door, we're professional," Scott recalls his coworker saying. Scott's pal also showed him the Amway Rules, the list of do's and don'ts that Van Andel and DeVos came up with during their FTC case, which were clearly accepted by the government as proof Amway wasn't an illegal pyramid scheme.

It all sounded legitimate to Scott—after all, this guy he knew and respected claimed he was raking it in, so it was certainly worth giving it a shot, right? If it worked for this guy, why couldn't it work for him? Scott bought in for roughly $150, which got him some training materials and products to try. Scott says he was unimpressed, mostly due to how expensive the products were. Amway's dish detergent, Crystal Bright, was four times the price of Palmolive's. Amway also sold a $600 vacuum cleaner, quite a pretty penny in 1993.[1] Today, for example, Amway sells sixty dishwasher tablets for $19.50 plus shipping.[2] That's thirty-two cents per tablet, about 50 percent more than Cascade pods, which you can get at the store or via Amazon Prime.[3] Amway also sells 112 loads' worth of nonchlorine laundry bleach for $27.[4] In comparison, 108 loads of OxiClean costs half that.[5]

But the prices didn't stop Scott from trying to make a go of it. After all, his upline threw around buzzwords such as *biodegradable* and told him the business was foolproof. They said that because they sold household items, people would buy no matter what, and because the products were so special, there would always be a market for Amway goods. According to Scott, Amway even had a shorthand term for this: *Amway money.* If someone is going to spend money on *something*, why not on Amway?

One of the first red flags that Scott saw but chose to ignore came during his initial training. "Buy from yourself first and teach others to do the same" was the mantra that sticks in Scott's head. It meant that if you're going to buy something anyway, *you*, the distributor, should be your first retail customer. This advice struck Scott as odd not only because you're not actually buying from yourself, you're buying from Amway, but also because it was so clearly teaching him how to run an illegal scam. If you're the seller and the end consumer, Amway is making all the money it needs off you. No mention was made of how to effectively sell products to outside customers, Scott says, only how to recruit others who would fill their own homes with Amway junk. But because the presentation was so breezy and the guy making it promised Scott he could bring in a few thousand dollars a month if he followed this advice, he went for it.

Immediately, he began to lose money; no one wanted his expensive soap. So he took his concerns to his upline and they said, "The reason you're not selling detergent is because you don't have these skills that we're going to give you in this tool." Unbeknownst to Scott when he signed up, a huge part of Amway's business comes in the form of "tools": tapes and classes and books and conferences that provide inspiration to struggling Amway sellers. But these are not free, unlike most job training in the mainstream marketplace. And they're so necessary, according to higher-ups, that most Amway sellers sign up for a monthly subscription and are automatically billed for these tools. When Scott pushed back ever so slightly—wondering exactly how necessary this additional expense was—his upline said, "The tools are optional, but so is success."

"You're constantly being encouraged. There's all this personal development going on that they're telling you about and how much they see you changing. And you hear how people struggle and struggle and struggle, and finally, you know, it just exploded in a good way. It was sort of like confirmation bias. 'Okay. This is happening to me, too. Just like everybody else.'"

The key to exploding in a good way? Scott says, "More tools. The answer to everything was to purchase more tools because any minute now things are gonna pick up."

Scott stayed the course for years. "I didn't really have time to slow down and think, and that's another one of their tricks, they keep you so busy. Between my job and raising two boys, church and recreation, you're just so busy that you don't think about it."

Then, in 2005, Scott's upline left the company and wrote a blog post bragging that he'd made $350,000 annually in his final years at Amway. A reader asked in the comments how much of that money was from selling tools, aka training materials, to his downline and how much from selling actual goods. The upline dodged the question for a number of exchanges, then finally caved: over half, he said.[6]

"I had an immediate reaction. . . . I thought, 'You guys

have been scamming me for a dozen years?' I mean, that was it." But Scott *still* didn't quit, he just decided to try to run a "clean" business and wrote a letter to one the founders of Amway, Rich DeVos, stating his intention to make the tools available on loan from his personal library for other Amway distributors. You know, to help struggling sellers and save them some money. Scott also went on a crusade to bust Amway sellers in the Houston area for breaking the Amway Rules. He says he knew of distributors who put Amway products on the shelves of brick-and-mortar stores and knew that recruiting was still the main thing anyone talked about at meetings. Every time he saw or heard something like this, he'd write a letter to corporate, sure they were unaware and not being willfully ignorant. Nothing was ever followed up on. "I wrote emails to Amway's complaint department starting in 2007 complaining about others cheating by advertising on Craigslist and eBay, and got *zero* meaningful responses, which caused me to start thinking Amway was not interested in enforcing their rules." Eventually, in 2009, Scott was terminated from the company for "being a nuisance," in his words. This isn't that uncommon, getting fired. It's a great strategy many MLMs deploy to keep people from speaking out against these schemes. Fall in line or get out.

When Scott sat down and took the time to do the math, to go over all of his books, he estimated that in the decade and a half he'd been with the company he'd lost around $200,000.

Which begs the question How? How, after nearly eight decades of MLM founders filling their coffers as 99 percent of their distributors lose money, do MLMs endure? Why, if most people lose money, do people still sign up? Why do so many people stay in so long when it clearly isn't working? Why do some of those same people then go on to join *different* MLMs? We know that, legally, MLMs won legitimacy in the United States after the FTC lost the Amway case in the late seventies, but this doesn't explain why the free market hasn't killed them. Shouldn't MLMs, given their increasingly tarnished reputation, be damaged goods?

There's no one answer to this, and as you dig deeper, you find that many of the assumed reasons are not always based in reality—or they only tell half the story. But seeking to understand also helps us understand some fundamental truths about human psychology and connection.

What of the Huns?

Despite the stereotype of the millennial housewife "hun" sliding into your DMs, the people who join MLMs come from all walks of life. For every former prom queen selling Arbonne, there's a Scott Johnson selling Amway or an undocumented Latinx immigrant selling Herbalife. Families in China and India are also selling Herbalife or Amway in the hopes of ascending into their countries' growing middle classes.

Though good data is hard to come by, the DSA does like to publish[7] a few stats about who signs up for MLMs in the United States. Mind you, all of these come from their own proprietary survey, so there's no way this is comprehensive or objective. In 2020, and using their verbiage, they said nearly 22 percent of all sellers in the United States were Hispanic. Eight percent were black. California, Texas, New York, and Florida were the biggest markets for MLMs. The picture the industry paints is of a diverse, urban sales force, comprising not just a bunch of Christian stay-at-home moms, but a multitude of disenfranchised Americans eager to make the American Dream their own.

The most objective survey of MLM participants was done in 2018 by AARP. It found that 40 percent of people who joined an MLM were working a full-time job and wanted to earn extra income; 16 percent were stay-at-home parents; 12 percent were students; and 11 percent were part-time employees looking to earn extra income. Almost *half* of first-time MLM participants were between ages eighteen and twenty-five. The average age of a first-time MLM participant was twenty-nine. Only one in four had any prior experience in sales where their income was primarily based on commissions.

Although the DSA and MLMs love to point out that every MLM seller has his or her own motivations for joining—for the friendship or the love of a product—this study showed that 90 percent of participants do intend to earn real money.[8]

Stacie Bosley, an economist and researcher at Hamline University and one of a small handful of academics studying MLMs, says[9] two types of people get into MLMs: "People who are experiencing financial insecurity and those with an 'identity deficit'—they see a gap between where they are in life and where they want to be." We keep talking about the fraud that MLMs bring upon individuals, but a larger fraud is perpetrated by our governments, our churches, our celebrities. It's that America is a meritocracy and that hard work and a good attitude are all you need to make it here. We've all bought in so completely that we can hardly tell the difference between working ourselves to death or working ourselves to a new life.

And there are many more reasons why someone might fall for the elusive promises of these companies despite the odds being stacked heavily against them.

For one thing, even though there is a ton of evidence that most MLM sellers don't make money or even lose money, you still have to search for that info and know where to look. That information is often in competition with the boosterism by the companies, which are usually not publicly traded and are therefore not required to open their books. The companies that do provide income disclosures often present them in a way that masks the reality. "They leave out, for example, the amount of people that make no check at all," Bosley says. "Which can often be seventy-five percent or more of the participants . . . and those people are not represented in an earnings table." The companies also usually only disclose gross revenues, not net profits, meaning they might tell you sellers receive a commission check of $1,000 a month without noting that those same sellers then use that money to buy more inventory, so they're left with nothing—and often, as in Scott's case, less than nothing.

Chances are, if you're considering joining an MLM, it's because someone is recruiting you using this misleading company data. That, coupled with what are likely enticing stories from the recruiters themselves, can be extremely persuasive when you're financially or spiritually in need. People who are savvy to pyramid schemes might stop here and say, "But all you have to do is some basic math to realize that this promise is BS!" As we've seen, if you work through the recruitment pattern, you'd run out of people on Earth to recruit within thirteen levels.[10] But somehow MLMs keep telling people this never-ending chain is totally possible, and not just possible, but necessary for success.

The problem is we humans are just really, really bad at doing this sort of exponential math, and so we don't immediately see why the recruiting structure is impossible even for people who got in right at the beginning. This is called the exponential growth bias and it's been studied for a long time.[11] One common question that illustrates how difficult this is to visualize goes like this: Would you rather have $1 million or a penny doubled every day for thirty days? So one penny becomes two on day two, four pennies on day three, and so on. Have your answer? Most people choose the million, but by doubling pennies for thirty days you'd end up with $5,368,709.12.[12]

In March 2021, a group of Israeli scholars aggregated many of these studies on exponential growth bias and found that "exponential progression does not appear to be part of the repertory of basic intuitions of the majority of individuals." This hole in our imagination is also the reason people get into credit card debt or fail to save enough money for retirement. The time it takes for someone to get into an MLM or a pyramid scheme, lose money, and leave is extended because we simply cannot comprehend what's possible, or impossible.

Bosley also points out that people interpret the MLM pitch very differently: "There's people who see the recruiting element and immediately think 'pyramid scheme' and go running. And there are people that hear the words *team building* and *entrepreneurship*, and that appeals to them. And so part of it is how you process the rhetoric."

This can be true even when both types of people are presented with the data that 99 percent of MLM participants don't make, and often lose, money on the endeavor. As a species, human beings are inclined to overweight small probabilities to help justify decisions. This is why people play the lotto even though their chances of winning are extremely slim. They think, "*Some*one is going to win. Why can't it be me?"

The probability of making money in an MLM is not the same for everyone. It's not based on chance but on mathematical feasibility, and no matter who you are, your chances of being in that 1 percent of MLMers who make money decline to essentially zero if you're late joining the scheme.

Companies don't present the stats this way, claiming instead that everyone has an equal opportunity but results depend on your character, outlook, and how hard you work. A small chance of success can motivate certain people, says Bosley. "I sat across from two students who were considering joining, and they had an income disclosure statement. It even said the percentage of people that earn zero dollars, and it was a lot. It was the majority. And one of the students looked at it and said, 'Oh my goodness. I don't want to do this. This looks like bad news,' and the other one looked at it and said, 'This is exactly why I want to do this. I want to prove that I belong in that group,' meaning the few winners, not the scores of losers."

Another thing MLMs have going for them is that many make the entry seem low risk. A lot less cash is on the line than in traditional businesses, which also have high rates of failure.

Besides, despite all the troubling news coming out of MLMs, they still benefit from the sheen of legitimacy given by the government. So even if you're aware that LuLaRoe has seen a lot of distributors jump ship, or that Wall Street has gone after Herbalife, it's easy for a different company to say, "That's not us. We're the good guys. This is what we do differently." The FTC says the companies are legal and distinguishes between legitimate business opportunities and pyramid schemes. Why not take a chance?

MLMs are not just promising wealth, but also freedom, community, and status. They're promising autonomy and empowerment and the realization of all your dreams. When you see your neighbor driving around in a brand-new SUV (allegedly) bought with an MLM commission check, it's easy to think, "Yeah, why not me? If they can do it, so can I."

"It really makes the traditional paths look a lot less interesting to a lot of people," Bosley says. "They start to believe that they don't want to go back to the nine-to-five. They don't want to go back to being locked down to a job and the old way of doing things. And it could change people in terms of what they expect, in terms of autonomy and the liberation that MLMs often promise."

Then there are all the social-status promises made particularly to women. Think of the #girlbosses and the #fempire and the stay-at-home mom who doesn't have time for a nine-to-five because she's busy with the kids. MLMs purportedly help you have it all: income, status, freedom.

According to that AARP study, at least 77 percent of people are recruited by someone they know: people were most likely to join an MLM if they were recruited by a friend (34 percent), followed by a coworker (12 percent), a neighbor (9 percent), and someone on social media (8 percent). An equal proportion (7 percent) of MLM distributors were recruited by someone from a religious organization and someone from a volunteer or community group.

Even if you don't know someone directly, you have a relationship with them through your existing network, which is all built on doing right by your neighbor and being honest. This is another reason why churches and schools are such active hunting grounds for new recruits: the organizations consist of like-minded individuals who share a common belief system that is, supposedly, built on the idea that hard work, kindness, and sharing will always pay off.

Randy Alcorn, the author of dozens of inspirational Christian books and founder of Eternal Perspective Ministries, wrote on his blog in 2019 about the proliferation of MLMs in his church community. He includes this anecdote as part cautionary tale:[13]

Years ago a woman visited our church one Sunday, took a church directory, and immediately started calling people straight down the list, offering her services with a particular multilevel sales company. When she called my wife, this woman shared how much she enjoyed our fellowship, saying that her family had decided ours would be their new church home. After some more pleasantries, she tried to sell her product. When my wife politely said she wasn't interested, the woman's previously sweet tone changed. She asked if there were others in the church already selling her product. When my wife said, "Yes, there's a number," there was a quiet "Oh," and the conversation ended. So did the relationship with our church.

Why Do People Stay?

Okay, so this (sort of) explains why people might decide to join an MLM despite all the red flags, but why do people stay, especially when they start losing money? The answer to this question provides a crash course in the illogical nature of human psychology.

You join, you spend a few thousand bucks on inventory and other expenses. You build your downline and start receiving some checks. It all looks great, but then you use that money to buy more product or to attend the annual sellers conference or, as Scott did, purchase a bunch of self-help materials that will supposedly take your business to the next level. Plus, you have to consider any other expenses—such as the cost to deliver or ship any product you sell, overhead costs such as your internet, cell phone, gas—perhaps even rent storage if you need to stock a lot of inventory. Wouldn't reasonable people stop after they do this and realize they're not making any money? Not necessarily.

By the time you do realize you're not making anything, you might feel that you're in too deep. You've spent so much time and money trying to make this venture work that now you need to keep working to, at the very least, make back your investment. This is something all humans do. We do not like to lose, so we will avoid losing even if we've already lost and it just means we'll lose more. Two related psychological phenomena are behind this: honoring sunk costs and loss aversion, and they are fascinating and something we all do whether we're involved with an MLM or not.

Honoring sunk costs is the idea that if we invest time, energy, money, or some other resource on something, we're inclined to keep investing in it even if it's not producing a return because we don't want to "lose" our investment. It's why people continue to gamble when they're in the hole. It's why you go on that couples retreat you planned months ago even though your honey left you for someone else a week before you were set to leave. It's why you follow through with the wedding when you've just been cheated on. It's why MLM sellers will convince themselves that if they just buy more inventory, spend a little more money, invest more time in recruiting, it will make all their earlier efforts pay off. And most of the time, we end up losing more resources because we hate the idea of losing resources.

A cousin to this phenomenon is loss aversion, which is exactly what it sounds like—an aversion to losing things. We don't like to lose so we will put off acknowledging that we've lost for as long as possible, even if we've already lost. The second MLM sellers say "I quit" is the second they have to accept that they have spent a bunch of time and money that they'll never get back on something that wasn't worth it. As long as they stay in the game, they still have a chance of turning things around—at least that's what they tell themselves.

If you look at a list of logical fallacies we all engage in, it almost reads like a list of qualifications to join an MLM. There's *ad fidentia*, which is when you respond to a challenge or personal attack with fervor to prove the person wrong. There's *affirming the consequent*, which is when you assume something will go wrong for a specific reason, then it does go wrong, and you assume it's for the reason you'd already landed on prior to failing. "My upline says I don't have enough inventory to make a good profit at this party. Oh, look, I didn't make a profit. It must be because my inventory is low," and not that the products are overpriced crap.

The *alphabet soup* fallacy is *all over* the network marketing world. This is the one that says fancy words and official-sounding acronyms add legitimacy to a pitch. In Amway's training packet, they explain how you can figure out what your commission might be:

1. **Personal Calculation:** Your personal BV times your PV bracket percent (based on your total PV, including pass-up).
2. **Differential Calculation:** The group BV of each of your frontline IBOs, times your PV bracket percent minus that IBO's PV bracket percent. (Differential is calculated separately for each of your frontline IBOs.)[14]

BV stands for "business volume" and *PV* means "point value," and *frontlines* are I don't know and same with *pass-ups*. Make sense? No. But it sounds like . . . something legitimate?

Then there are the lists of things a recruiter can do to try to sway our decision-making so we're not basing things on logic. These are appeals to emotions or how we feel about a certain celebrity or how we're all in this together or how much we *deserve* this opportunity.

Those things are true of basically every economic proposition, and all of us succumb to a logical fallacy at some point.

But MLMs operate in ways that, once you realize your logical error, make them particularly hard to leave.

First is the community aspect and group dynamics— feeling that if you leave, you'll disappoint everyone or have no friends. This happened to Scott when he asked his upline to stop his tools subscription—they went from talking almost every day to radio silence. It's a cliché to compare MLMs to cults, but the worst of them *do* behave a lot like cults in how they treat their members. Steven Hassan is an expert in what makes an organization a cult, and to help you determine if you're encountering one, he has a handy acronym, *BITE*: Behavioral control, Information control, Thought control, Emotional control.[15]

Culty groups start by making you feel that you're part of something bigger than yourself: this group is not just about selling essential oils, it's about helping people and lifting one another up and saving lives. It's not just about makeup, it's about providing a stay-at-home mom the money she needs to treat herself to something nice. The cosmetics MLM LimeLife preaches that all you need to do to achieve success is "share." "We're not salespeople, we're shares people," the owner, Michele Gay, preaches in a Facebook Live video.

Jennifer Chatman, a UC Berkeley Hass School of Business professor who studies corporations and organizational culture, told *Business Insider*[16] that MLMs and cults both recruit people based on relationships, and both MLMs and cults target people going through hardship. "They say, here's a person who is very similar to you, and you should forge a relationship with them and they're going to be really nice to you," Chatman said. "Even more than it being a job and a source of income, it's a source of relationship gratification. They feel an allegiance to one another and feel pressure to sell based on living up to their friendships with their peers within the organization."

Since you've been recruited by someone you know and are recruiting people you know, you typically feel responsible for them—quitting is not just quitting a job; it's betraying those closest to you. Some of this is just social dynamics—you don't like disappointing people—but some companies actively target sellers or former sellers who criticize or leave the company. In countless MLM training videos you can find on YouTube, you'll see uplines discouraging participants from communicating with critics, even if you were once friends. This is often bundled with a sour grapes theory: these people don't like the company because they couldn't be successful. Don't let them get too close or their bad vibes may rub off on you. What's actually accomplished is a narrowing of the blinders you have to wear to stay in the business.

Katie Heid, a former Mary Kay consultant from Michigan, said she was ostracized from everyone in her down- and uplines (except for her best friend, who had recruited her into the scheme). She didn't see it coming. "You keep hearing the same message over and over and over again. You become part of a family, and if you leave Mary Kay, we have a lot of people that went to Mary Kay Heaven. They just dropped off the radar and now we don't really spend any time with them anymore. That isn't how a business relationship should be. There are all sorts of businesses that part ways, but they're still useful to each other. Why wouldn't you keep that connection? There's none of that."

Then we have the founder worship. To hear how people talk about certain MLM founders, you'd imagine they were talking about their spiritual guru—not their boss. Keith Raniere—the now infamous (and incarcerated) founder of the self-help/sex-trafficking cult NXIVM—got his start in MLMs and instituted the same recruitment and retainment techniques in NXIVM that he'd used for those earlier ventures.

Beyond the cultlike atmosphere of most MLMs, connections have been drawn between them and conspiracy theories, such as QAnon. An October 2020 *Atlantic* article examined the prevalence of MLM participation of QAnon believers. "These are organizations built on foundational myths (that the establishment is keeping secrets from you, that you are on a hero's journey to enlightenment and wealth), charismatic leadership, and shameless, constant posting. The people at the top of them are enviable, rich, and gifted at wrapping everything that happens—in their personal lives, or in the world around them—into a grand narrative about how to become as happy as they are. In 2020, what's happening to them is dark and dangerous, but it looks gorgeous."

Even if you're lucky to escape (or be immune to) the cult-like fanaticism and manipulation that can happen in MLMs, you might not want to quit because, well, quitting something that was sold to you as your one opportunity to have financial freedom sucks. People don't like to feel like failures, and MLMs are good at making you feel like a failure—the only way to fail is to quit; you're so close; if you quit now, you'll miss out on the big break you've been working toward all these years.

What Happens After?

Some people see the truth behind the gaslighting and realize that they've been set up to fail—that no matter how hard they try, they will never be a millionaire because the math just doesn't add up. They could be the world's greatest salespeople, but you can't sell your way through the laws of economics. You can't make money selling something if you and your downline are the only ones buying it. You can only recruit so many people until you run out of customers.

But then you have to deal not only with the impact this has had on you and your financial situation, but also the impact this has had on your recruits. None want to feel that they've been duped, but you also don't want to acknowledge that, no matter how inadvertently, you've duped other people. It's one of the most insidious aspects of this model: the minute you recruit a new person, you're in on the scam.

Even if people realize they've been duped, they might not want to admit it—even if they leave, they are often reticent to talk about their experience—or they rationalize it, e.g., "Well, I wasn't really trying to make money; I just wanted to buy product." Of all the corporate complaints of fraud that flow into the FTC, MLMs don't even make the top ten according to Bosley. Folks on the inside, those with the bad experiences, are just not talking as loudly as you'd expect. This resistance to talking about it is probably why the MLMs persist—the info is out there, but not as widely available as you might believe. This perpetuates a cycle wherein the people most able to explain the dark side of MLMs are usually not inclined to do so, so the information isn't as widespread.

Also, people are more likely to participate in fraud if they've seen someone else participate—though it seems as if the opposite should be true.[17] If you know someone who did LuLaRoe and then quit but didn't tell you the story, then you might decide to sign up because, well, this reasonable person gave it a shot.

The very existence of MLMs, that the government has signed off on them, creates a hugely false sense of security.

Maybe the answer is that MLMers *just want to believe.*
They want to believe that, if they just work hard and do a
good job, they can be successful. They want to believe that
people are honest and want to help them. They want to believe that they are intelligent and capable of achieving success.
They want to believe you can balance family responsibilities
while supporting yourself financially. And why not, when
you consider the alternatives. The rise in information about
how dangerous MLMs are has also sort of paralleled a decline in opportunity—everything seems like a fraud or a lot
of effort. Even getting a college degree isn't worth your time
and money any longer. It's mostly people in their twenties
who join MLMs. These are the Gen Zers and millennials,
who, study after study has shown, are the first generations in
modern American history to be worse off than their parents,
yet they're the self-esteem generations, who were taught they
could do anything if they just put their mind to it. So why
amass hundreds of thousands of dollars in student loan debt
to get a minimum-wage job or work for a corporation that
doesn't pay you a living wage or good benefits when you can
be "working for yourself" and making money talking to your
friends on social media?

Which brings us to loneliness. According to a survey con-
ducted in October 2020 by researchers at Harvard's Making
Caring Common Project, 36 percent of adults reported feeling lonely "frequently" or "almost all the time or all the time"

in the previous month, right in the thick of the pandemic. This included 61 percent of young people aged eighteen to twenty-five and 51 percent of mothers with young children. About half of lonely young adults in the survey reported that no one in the past few weeks had "taken more than just a few minutes" to ask how they were doing in a way that made them feel as if the person "genuinely cared." That's never the case in an MLM; even though the check-ins from your upline are financially motivated, that call may be better than no call at all.

10

Why Isn't Anyone Doing Anything?

et's review. MLMs make money by telling people they can strike it rich through an amazing opportunity to sell an incredible product. But instead of simply paying people a commission or wage to sell those products to consumers (as in a traditional retail operation), MLMs encourage sellers to consistently recruit new sellers (aka their downline) by offering them a commission on any of their recruits' sales. The more product they and their downline sell, the higher their discounts on any products they purchase directly, and the higher their standing within the company. MLM leaders also preach that sellers should look at every potential customer as a potential recruit. Thus, over time, the customers and sellers become indistinguishable from one another, and the market in their area gets saturated because everyone is selling to everyone else and there is no one left to recruit. To earn commissions and keep their standing within the company, sellers either have to convince their downlines to buy more product to have on hand to sell (to whom?) or buy the product themselves for "personal use." When sellers eventually realize they're not making any money because they keep reinvesting their commissions into purchasing more inventory they can't sell, they're told they're not working hard enough and lack a winner's mindset. So they keep investing more money into inventory, classes, retreats, and other tools that promise to teach them how to be better entrepreneurs but actually just rehash what they already know. While early recruits with massive downlines can make tons of money, the vast majority of sellers lose money and eventually quit, go into debt, or both.

Under the FTC's guidelines, the only thing that distinguishes an MLM from a pyramid scheme is sales of a product or service to an end consumer. But since, as we've seen, the end consumer and seller are often the same person, the vast majority of MLMs end up being pyramid schemes. This, coupled with the other sketchy behaviors these companies engage in—claiming their unique blend of essential oils can cure Alzheimer's and cancer, encouraging sellers to buy new cars, pricey vacations, and other things they can't afford and post about it on social media, misrepresenting earnings claims, and all manner of other nonsense—leaves us wondering, How in the hell do these companies continue to exist with seemingly no consequences?

For example, as of this writing, LuLaRoe continues to operate despite a huge public shaming and a couple of high-profile losses in courts. The FTC sued Herbalife while one of the world's richest and most powerful men, Bill Ackman, shorted the company's stock while trying to expose it as a fraud. Yet the company still earns billions of dollars in net revenue, in the United States and abroad, every year. Amway is still convincing people to sign up to shill soap for them while promising them they can strike it rich and live the American Dream—even if they live in China or Russia. Shall I go on? Sure, a few companies have been successfully prosecuted for fraud. Some have been forced to shut down. But the MLM industry is still going strong with few signs of slowing down.

So how can we stop it?

The most obvious way to go after an MLM would be to prove it's a pyramid scheme in federal court. That despite its claims to the contrary, most people have no feasible way to make money through retail sales. If you can prove that most of a company's sales are to other sellers, then you prove the company is illegal based on the FTC's definition.

Unfortunately, to do this is not so straightforward. First, you'd have to do it for every company, one by one. Because the current law protects the MLM industry's definition of their business structure, most MLMs are able to distance themselves from other MLMs that have been prosecuted for fraud by saying, "Oh, but we're not like them!" Currently, around 130 companies[1] are members of the DSA, a small fraction of the industry in the United States, and more MLMs enter the market regularly. Evidence shows that people who quit an MLM usually just join another one, so eliminating just one MLM at a time does little to protect most consumers in the long run.

Okay, so it's hard work, but isn't protecting consumers from scammy businesses the FTC's entire job? Yes, but going after hundreds of companies one at a time requires resources. The FTC marshaled a ton of resources to go after Amway in the 1970s and still lost.

Even though it's supposed to be a big scary government agency, the FTC is actually no match, in resources, to the most successful MLMs. The FTC's budget in 2021 was $351 million,[2] and that's for everything. "Basically they're in charge of supervising the entire economy of the United States," says John Breyault, a vice president at the consumer watchdog group the National Consumers League. "They could be a ten-billion-dollar-a-year agency and still not have enough money to go after all the companies that are under their supervision."[3]

This one agency alone is responsible for identifying and prosecuting credit card fraud, stolen identities, catfishing, false product claims and snake-oil sales, telemarketing fraud, all of those phony texts you get about Netflix overcharging you or the IRS needing you to contact them at some obscure website to pay an outstanding bill. I could keep going; this is but a small fraction of the FTC's mandate. Meanwhile, in 2020, thirty-four separate DSA members had global revenues[4] in excess of $351 million. Sixteen of them, including Amway, Herbalife, Tupperware (yes, Tupperware), Young Living, and Usana, had revenues of more than $1 billion. To further frustrate matters, the FTC only has the authority to bring civil lawsuits, not criminal ones. The best the agency can do is financially disrupt a business or force it into bankruptcy. Even in successful prosecutions, no one goes to jail.

When I spoke with someone at the agency recently, she kept referring to the current "target-rich environment." At first, I assumed she meant that there were too many MLMs and other fraudulent companies for the FTC to target efficiently, so it had to be strategic about how it used its resources. But after a while, I realized I had it wrong. She clarified that the "targets" she was referring to weren't companies, but consumers. Too many of us poor suckers are susceptible to fraud. And it's not even our fault. In a world where wages are stagnant but the cost of living keeps rising, where younger generations are struggling to achieve the same standard of living their parents did, where we've just survived a global pandemic and are reckoning with climate change, well, who can blame us for being a little tired, desperate, and lonely? All the things we were told would bring us wealth and health and happiness—going to college, getting a job, buying a home, living the American Dream—haven't worked. So why not try something new? Especially if it comes with girls' nights out and cute makeup at a discount!

The FTC has to pick and choose what to spend its money on, so it's only going to pick cases it thinks it can win. From 1997 to 2005 it received 17,858 complaints against pyramid schemes but prosecuted fewer than 20.[5] The evidence the FTC has to gather to prove its case against an MLM includes everything from the amount of money individual sellers have lost as a result of their participation (which, as we've seen, many people have trouble realizing, let alone admitting), as well as proof that the company lied about potential earnings in an effort to recruit sellers (which is complicated by the fact that MLM executives can deny responsibility for a pitch made by a seller). Even so, when the FTC does bring a lawsuit, it wins. According to researcher William Keep, the FTC has won every pyramid scheme case it has fought since the 1990s. In addition to the companies the agency successfully targets, many would-be defendants choose to go out of business rather than face the government in court.[6]

Because most MLMs are privately held and therefore not required to disclose their financial or operating information publicly, the government relies on consumers to file complaints before it has cause to investigate a particular company. And because the FTC has to be so selective about the cases it takes on, it typically needs a lot of complaints before it pays attention. In the most high-profile pyramid scheme case of the past decade, Herbalife—a publicly traded, massive MLM that had a remarkable number of complaints against it—avoided a judgment by paying a $200 million settlement. When you consider Herbalife's net revenues that year, $4.5 billion,[7] and that the settlement had to be split among 350,000 victims— just shy of $600 apiece—you see how the FTC's wins often look like losses.[8]

Settlements are not nothing, but by design they allow the companies to keep operating. A settlement often requires a company to cede something—admitting to wrongdoing or changing its business practices to avoid whatever "mistakes" it made. The biggest problem is that the agreements require enforcement to be effective in the long term. For instance, the FTC instructed Herbalife in its settlement to "restructure its business so that participants are rewarded for what they sell, not how many people they recruit." "Herbalife is going to have to start operating legitimately, making only truthful claims about how much money its members are likely to make," said then FTC chairwoman Edith Ramirez. "It will have to compensate consumers for the losses they have suffered as a result of what we charge are unfair and deceptive practices."[9] But again, the only thing the FTC has the ability to do is collect consumer complaints. It doesn't send someone around to knock on Herbalife distributors' doors preemptively or show up at the company's headquarters for a meeting with its accountant. And even if the FTC did, Herbalife is a global company, with most of its sales occurring outside the United States. In 2021, for example, 75 percent of Herbalife's $5.8 billion in net global revenues came from abroad.[10] Even if things change here, they don't have to change in other markets. And how would we know if they did?

Then there is the problem of political will. The FTC chairperson is appointed by the president, which means the FTC's mandate, priorities, and agenda change frequently and typically complement those of whatever party holds the Oval Office. A business-friendly administration with a laissez-faire attitude toward corporate regulation and a love for consumer "choice" and "freedom" is likely not going to spend tax dollars on prosecuting wealthy business owners, especially if, ahem, the politicians know those business owners personally, as we saw with Gerald Ford and Amway. But MLMs have found allies among both parties.

The Amway decision was handed down in 1979. Under that decision, the FTC refused to call Amway a pyramid scheme because it sold a product that filled a market need. (One could argue that Amway was not filling any need by selling cleaners when one could purchase a like or better version for less money at any grocery store in town, but I digress.) Many former Amway sellers and many economic and legal experts argue that Amway cannot make money through retail sales alone, especially now that the market is so saturated, but the FTC would need to prove that to bust the company. At the time of this decision, there weren't that many MLMs, so if the government had enforced this rule in the 1980s, Amway might have been shut down and the industry would not have flourished. But that is not what happened.

In 1980, Ronald Reagan was elected president on a platform of trickle-down economics and deregulation—the same economic principles the DeVos and Van Andel families had been supporting for decades. Amway loved Reagan. Van Andel and DeVos were the biggest individual backers of Reagan's campaign.[11] The duo dined with the secretary of state, Alexander Haig, at the opening of the Gerald R. Ford Museum, to which they donated $200,000, and later hired Haig to consult for them on their international expansion efforts.[12]

Rich DeVos led the Republican Party's Congressional Leadership Council and was so successful he became the finance chair of the Republican National Committee in 1981. (He was removed a year later after praising the "cleansing" qualities of the recession and bashing unions.)[13]

The duo spent hundreds of thousands of dollars on Reagan's reelection campaign, and the president won his second term in 1984.[14] Amway then invited Reagan to give a speech at their annual convention one day after his inauguration.

Reagan staffers worried about the optics of the president appearing to endorse the organization so publicly, so the event was rebranded as an "homage to an ideal that both [Amway and the president] embrace." Amway later sold tapes of Reagan's speech at the renamed "Spirit of America Salute to Free Enterprise" event for $37 as part of their internal promotional materials.[15] The trio were so chummy that, in 1987, the president even appointed DeVos to his AIDS task force, where, according to DeVos's own later recollections, he "listened to three hundred witnesses tell us that it was everybody else's fault but their own [that they contracted the disease]."[16] Charming.

The next administration was a litte less showy with its ties to MLMs, that is until the year after President George H. W. Bush left office and set a record for the most money accepted by a former president—$100,000—for a speech he made, at an Amway convention.[17]

The Clinton administration was a little more subdued in its publicized ties to MLMs, but a generally laissez-faire attitude toward the industry still prevailed and it was allowed to proliferate. In one of the more bizarre anecdotes of twentieth-century political history I came across in researching this book, Madeline Albright, a few years after leaving her position as Clinton's secretary of state, became a brand ambassador for Herbalife. Between 2008 and 2014, she earned an estimated $10 million for her role.[18]

After the Clinton presidency, in 2001, things took a hard right turn when newly elected president George W. Bush appointed Timothy Muris as FTC chairman. Muris had held various other positions at the commission earlier in his career, but just prior to his appointment, he worked at a law firm that represented, among its largest clients, Amway. Following his work for the Bush administration, Muris, along with J. Howard Beales (whom Muris had appointed to head Consumer Protection), became lobbyists for the MLM industry.[19]

Then, toward the end of the Bush years, the FTC proposed a rule that would likely have rendered it impossible for MLMs to recruit new members. First proposed in 2006, the Business Opportunity Rule was designed to protect consumers from "bogus business opportunities" by requiring companies offering at-home moneymaking schemes to disclose certain pertinent information to potential recruits. This included such things as proof that real people had earned decent money on this opportunity and whether the company had faced any legal trouble.

Spotting an existential threat, the DSA leaped into battle mode and began aggressively lobbying the commission to exempt MLMs from the rule. The FTC received seventeen thousand letters in defense of MLMs, including a few from sympathetic elected officials, and just two hundred from MLM opponents.[20]

The effort paid off. When the rule was finalized in 2011,

under the administration of George W.'s successor, Barack Obama, MLMs were exempt. Thanks to this, more MLMs, including the now-notorious LuLaRoe, which launched in 2012, brazenly came on the scene.

Then came Donald Trump. It's no secret that Trump loves anything that can make him money. MLMs are no exception. Trump had a personal MLM, which he bought in 2009, renamed the Trump Network, and sold in 2012 for an unknown amount.[21] The company, which sold vitamins and supplements (classic!), was so often accused of being a pyramid scheme that high-level distributors at the company taught lower-level recruits handy comebacks to use as defense. "What's a pyramid scheme?" one Diamond Director seller queried a roomful of Trump Network recruits at a 2011 seminar. "Like the food pyramid? Like the Catholic Church? What about where you work? If you ask me, corporate America is a pyramid scheme. All the people on the top make all the money. The people at the bottom are spinning their wheels." He added, "You think Donald Trump would involve himself in a pyramid scheme?"[22]

In addition to profiting, however briefly, from his own MLM, Trump earned $8.8 million from American Communications Network, an MLM that sells internet and phone services, between 2005 and 2015. In exchange, Trump heavily promoted ACN's services and, more important, its "business opportunity," including through his hit reality show *The*

Apprentice. Based on his endorsement, would-be millionaires paid thousands of dollars registering to sell ACN's services, primarily landline videoconferencing—in the midaughts—only to lose it all when they realized the opportunity was a fraud.[23]

Trump also curried favor with GOP fan favorite Amway by appointing Betsy DeVos, the wife of former Amway CEO Richard DeVos Jr. and daughter-in-law of Amway founder Richard DeVos Sr., to secretary of education. After decades of political maneuvering and more than $82 million in donations since 1999 alone,[24] the DeVos family finally had a seat in the federal government it had, for so long, despised. Plus, as education secretary, Betsy would be able to advocate policy and programs that could potentially weaken America's public education system for good. A boon for Christian conservatism and free enterprise indeed!

What about the states?

The Feds aren't the only people with authority to go after questionable businesses. States have jurisdiction, too, and many of them have laws on the books that prohibit or greatly curtail MLM activity. In some cases, states have pioneered legislation to help protect consumers from similar scams. The first real anti-pyramid-scheme legislation came in 1968 when California passed its "endless chain" statute. The law defines an "endless chain" the same way we now define a pyramid scheme and criminalizes anyone who sets one up.[25] Other states have laws that regulate specific MLM behavior, for example by requiring companies to buy back unwanted inventory or prohibiting them from claiming sellers can earn a specific amount of money by selling their products.[26]

But states face many—if not more—of the same challenges the FTC does. They, too, have limited resources to undertake years-long investigations, and because their jurisdiction is limited, the most they can do is influence how a company operates within their state. For example, when LuLaRoe settled the case brought against them by the Washington State Attorney General's Office, it agreed to adhere to specific guidelines in the state going forward. These included such things as calculating bonuses on actual retail sales, instead of sales to other retailers, and allowing retailers to return inventory for a full refund within forty-five days of signing up. LuLaRoe also agreed to pay a $4.75 million fine, $4 million of which the state would use to compensate three thousand former retailers in the state.[27] When one considers that, according to the company's disclosures, more than sixty thousand sellers left the company between 2017 and 2021 alone, one sees how little of an impact this settlement has made on the rest of LuLaRoe's disillusioned seller base.[28]

At the state level, lawsuits against businesses are handled by the attorney general's office. Many states have taken action against MLMs, but many others have not. In some cases, the very people responsible for prosecuting fraud are making it easier for MLMs to operate.

In 2015, while serving as attorney general for California, future vice president Kamala Harris declined to investigate Herbalife. This was after the FTC had opened its investigation, and other state attorneys general, including those in Illinois and New York, had brought their own cases against the company. It was also after prosecutors in Harris's own office requested resources to look into the company. They alleged the company had been ignoring an injunction the state had brought against it in 1986 that ordered it to stop making false earnings claims to potential recruits.[29]

It's unclear why Harris refused to take on what could have been a high-profile and potentially winnable case. Some aides say the 1986 injunction was too vague to be enforceable. Others in her office say she didn't want to take any action that would affect Herbalife's share price and therefore play into the public investing war between Bill Ackman and Carl Icahn. "We need to find out if Herbalife has violated the law," someone who worked closely with Harris told the *New York Times*, "but we should not go about our business of figuring that out in a way where we are being used to make one billionaire richer than another one."[30]

We do know that Harris's husband, Douglas Emhoff, worked at a law firm that represented Herbalife, and Harris had received donations from a lobbyist who was later hired by the company. The donations were only a few thousand dollars (hardly DeVos money), and there's no evidence that Emhoff worked directly with Herbalife. But the whole affair goes to show how difficult it can be to convince politicians to go after these companies—and how well-connected the industry is to political elites.

We've discussed Utah being an MLM safe haven, but it's far from alone in currying favor with the industry. As of 2022, twenty-eight states had passed similar antipyramid legislation thanks to the lobbying efforts of the DSA.[31] These laws make it even more difficult for states to bring cases against MLMs since they force them to prove a specific company is behaving like an illegal pyramid and not a "legitimate retail business."

Class-Action Inaction

Okay, so if you can't rely on the states and the Feds, what can you do? One solution is to get together with all of the other sellers who have been duped by a specific MLM and file a class-action lawsuit. In recent years, this has become a popular tactic. Between 2017 and 2021, twenty-nine federal class-action lawsuits were filed against various MLMs.[32]

Class-action lawsuits have many advantages. For one, they offer a recourse for individuals when they can't get justice via the government. The litigation also brings to light a lot of information about specific companies that may be difficult, if not impossible, to access otherwise. This gives journalists, academics, government watchdogs, and other observers the opportunity to bring any malfeasance to light for the general public, thus hopefully deterring would-be recruits from joining that particular MLM and losing their life savings.

But such lawsuits also have major downsides. For one thing, class-action cases require multiple individuals to come together to sue the company directly. This is a lengthy, tiresome process in the best scenarios, and that's if the plaintiffs can find an attorney willing to take on the case. But more important, according to one of the industry's most tireless critics, Robert FitzPatrick, these lawsuits don't lead to any meaningful change. MLMs basically consider lawsuits a cost of doing business and would rather settle than drag out the process in court. As part of these settlements, MLMs are required to pay a fine but are allowed to keep doing business, and the courts have no opportunity to deem them illegal or fraudulent, even if they are operating illegally or fraudulently. As long as they can keep making money to pay their legal fees, they can keep functioning the way they always have.[33]

Okay, this is all very depressing, but there is some good news. As more and more people have become aware of just how scammy MLMs are, the government is starting to take some action toward thwarting them.

The most significant of these moves comes back to the FTC's Business Opportunity Rule, which was passed in 2011 with a major exception for the MLM industry. In June 2021, the FTC announced it would review the rule as part of its ten-year-review plan. In the announcement, Commissioner Rohit Chopra urged that the commission include multi-level marketing (along with other industries that rely on an independent labor force such as gig-economy platforms) in the rule's provisions going forward.[34] If the government changes the rule, it would require MLMs to be honest about how much money sellers earn, which would eliminate their main recruitment tool. If they can no longer promise people easy wealth on their own terms, what do they have to offer except overpriced makeup and questionable diet products?

The FTC *has* recently won a few lawsuits against MLMs, charging them with being illegal pyramid schemes. In one lawsuit, filed in early 2022,[35] FTC chairman Sam Levine said a "phony credit repair" scheme had bilked customers out of $213 million since 2015. Based in Michigan, it went by a few names, including Financial Education Services and United Wealth Services. The scheme operated mostly through telemarketing and websites: representatives would call up targets and pitch them a service to clean up their credit scores using a variety of methods. The reps said they could get dings removed from your credit report. The reps said they'd send the customers' information on rent payments on their homes to credit-reporting bureaus to show the customers' were in good standing with their landlords. But that info isn't really used by credit bureaus when determining credit scores. Many "customers" were charged $99 up front for this service and sometimes kept paying monthly fees regardless of whether the credit-improvement promise was kept. The reps even promised they could get participants new lines of credit, thus upping their score (they couldn't).

"Attention!! If you have 400–500 credit score and want a 700–800 score, I have a connection that legally erases negative things. repos, foreclosures, late payments, medical, student loans, evictions, and more," read one social media post from a representative. Scripts with unsubstantiated claims from supposed former clients asserted such things as "When I started in the service I had a low 500 credit score and within six months it jumped to over 700 and I was able to purchase a new Mercedes-Benz!" Not surprisingly, COVID was also used: agents would sympathize with potential marks, explaining that credit scores went down for most people during this time, so they were far from alone.

But the main thing that got the company in trouble, and that won the FTC its case before the U.S. District Court in Eastern Michigan, was that the company was *also* operating as a pyramid scheme.

On the phone with people who were already struggling financially—otherwise why would they need the credit repair service?—agents would pitch the opportunity for these people to make these calls themselves, sometimes promising upward of $1,000 a week in income by "building a team." When you look at the lawsuit, it's easy to spot the pyramid scheme because it works exactly as in most multi-level marketing schemes. Reading through the lawsuit is frustrating when you imagine inserting a different name for the accused party in paragraphs such as these:

> Defendants purport to pay what they call a "customer acquisition bonus" or "CAB" that is generated when an FES Agent enrolls a new agent. "Agents" typically receive a CAB of $100, "field trainers" receive $160, "senior field trainers" receive $240, and "pinnacle senior vice presidents" receive $560. Another bonus is called the "infinity bonus" that starts for FES Agents who rise to the "sales director" level. The infinity bonus is a percentage of the revenue brought in by the FES Agent's entire downline.

> Defendants and their agents often encourage FES Agents to "sponsor" new recruits, *i.e.*, if a potential recruit is unwilling to pay the $288 sign-up fee, the FES Agent should pay some or all of those fees on the recruit's behalf in order to inflate artificially the original FES Agent's downline and qualify the FES Agent for bonuses or other compensation.

I mean, yeah, that's how MLMs work! The FTC has been successful since this win in shutting down a few more of these credit repair schemes, though none as large as Financial Education Services.

Another recent win was against a health-and-wellness MLM called AdvoCare. After proving it was a pyramid scheme, the FTC forced AdvoCare to return $149 million to victims—or colluders, depending on how you look at it—of which there were more than two hundred thousand. If each of them made a claim, they'd get about $750 back.

As you know, the pyramid scheme angle is tough to prove, and I'd argue that, at least in the case of FES, it was an easier win because the service FES was selling was completely bogus, nonexistent. Not so easy when actual vitamins and supplements and leggings are being produced. So the FTC refocused its efforts on companies making false marketing claims. Similar to the letters sent out in 2020 to dōTERRA and others who made false statements about how their products could cure or prevent COVID, in early 2023 the commission issued 690 warning letters to businesses who might—or might not!—be making unsubstantiated claims about their customers' experiences. A company could not be "falsely claiming an endorsement by a third party; misrepresenting that an endorsement represents the experience or opinions of product users; misrepresenting that an endorser is an actual, current, or recent user of a product or service; continuing to use an endorsement without good reason to believe that the endorser continues to hold the views presented; using an endorsement to make deceptive performance claims; failing to disclose an unexpected material connection with an endorser; and misrepresenting that the experience of endorsers are typical or ordinary. Note that positive consumer reviews are a type of endorsement, so such reviews can be unlawful if they are fake or if a material connection is not adequately disclosed." Violate any of these rules and your firm could face a civil penalty of around $50,000. Which is great, but again, not that big of a dent. And those letters didn't *just* go to MLMs; it didn't even go out to *most* MLMs. Of the nearly seven hundred letters sent, around one hundred were to multi-level marketing schemes; many were to companies such as Walmart and Jessica Alba's Honest Company and, you guessed it, Gwyneth Paltrow's Goop.[36]

A tiny but interesting bit about this latest effort: in a dissenting opinion one of the commissioners wrote that sending the letters was stupid. On the eve of her resignation from the commission, Trump appointee Christine Wilson—also a close colleague and supporter of Ted Cruz—issued a letter in which she complained, "I am wary of a 13(b) fix that would afford the Commission significant latitude to seek equitable monetary relief in all substantiation cases, many of which involve complex and nuanced issues and dueling experts." In other words, it's too hard to prove that these companies are doing bad stuff, so why bother sending a letter?[37]

One does wonder how this would be enforced—especially since a company can just blame its individual sellers for misrepresentation and the FTC would most likely remain underresourced. There is a universe where some U.S. administration comes along and decides enough is enough, that the evidence proves unequivocally that these schemes are scams, and the whole practice is abolished—in the United States—a ban that would not likely extend across the globe. I hate to end this all on a super-downer note, but if I'm being honest with myself, I don't think that would stop the types of people who want to run these companies, people who knowingly bankrupt young moms, for example. I don't think anything would stop that kind of personality from finding a dubious way to squeeze the last few dollars out of any pockets they can get their hands into.

Jennifer Rajala became a social worker at Children's Protective Services (CPS) in Michigan in 2012. She'd grown up similar to the way I had, moving from a small town in Minnesota to an even smaller town in Michigan's Upper Peninsula in junior high. Her parents owned a Laundromat and a car wash and things were comfortable and boring, just what most people want out of a small-town existence. As she got ready to graduate from high school, she wasn't sure what she wanted to do with her life, but she knew it had to have something to do with helping people. So, she applied and got into Michigan State University—the university that gets in the news a lot for having a good men's basketball team and a seething rivalry with the University of Michigan, where my parents went.

After getting a degree in social work and criminal justice, Jennifer eventually moved back to her hometown of Crystal Falls, which is smack-dab in the middle of nowhere, but you can get to three of the Great Lakes in just a few hours. The town is tiny—only around fifteen hundred people live there, most of them white, most of them baby boomers, but with some small families such as Jennifer's. She married the brother of her best friend from high school, and they now have three little girls—a perfect small-town love story.

When she first started working for CPS, Jennifer said it was stressful but had a lot of benefits. First, it was a government job so there were good literal benefits, but it also gave her that sense of doing good she was looking for, and it earned her a decent living in an area without a lot of economic opportunity. But then came what I'll call the Bad Case, which derailed her, taking her out of social work and into multi-level marketing.

On the morning of June 24, 2014, just a few towns over from Crystal Falls, a mother dropped off her three-month-old daughter and two-year-old son at their babysitter's. The babysitter's own three-year-old son was also in the home. The babysitter said she stepped outside to take the trash out and smoke a cigarette, and when she came back inside, something was wrong with the baby, she seemed to have injured her head somehow. The babysitter called 911, and the baby was taken to a hospital but died three days later of blunt-force trauma, similar to the injury we all know as shaken baby syndrome. The babysitter was charged with murder, but a jury found her not guilty, instead believing the story the suspect told authorities: one of the boys had either jumped on the baby inside her playpen or dropped her on her head while the babysitter had stepped away. One of those authorities was Jennifer. The ordeal broke Jennifer's heart and resolve, and serendipitously—or perhaps intentionally during this time of immense stress—a friend introduced Jennifer to Arbonne, the beauty and wellness MLM. "She knew that I was about to have a baby, and she knew that I had an emotionally stressful job because I had complained about it on Facebook, where she sent me the message. But she was very new with her opportunity, so I don't hold any of this against her."

Jennifer said her skin was in terrible shape and the products her friend gifted her from Arbonne actually worked, clearing up her skin and making her feel better. Upon receiving this positive response, the friend pitched the real opportunity to Jennifer: selling the products herself. Thinking she needed an escape from CPS and that this might be at the very least a light and fun thing to do while she was having her second child, Jennifer signed on.

She says her first big introduction came during what Arbonne calls a "third-party call," in which the recruiter and recruit chat with someone way higher up at the company about what's possible by joining. "She asked me, what's your vision for your life? What's your five-year plan? Well, wouldn't you want to be a present mom? Would it be useful for you to bring in more income for your family? And do you enjoy your job? What about your job do you not like? What *do* you like? And I said, 'I love helping people.' And, of course, that was something that was like, 'Oh, well, the way we look at this opportunity is, it's a way to help people beyond just your small town.'" The woman also claimed to have left a job on Wall Street to sell Arbonne full-time. In retrospect, Jennifer realizes she should've asked more questions like "What exactly was this Wall Street job?," but she was so dazzled, she just caved to the pitch.

"There was an emphasis on perhaps people in small towns not being very big thinkers. And what would it mean to me to be around people who thought bigger, not only for themselves, but for me. And I felt like, 'Yeah, I want to do more. I want to have more, be more.' At that time in my life, all of those things sounded really great," Jennifer recalls. "It's pitched like a legitimate business opportunity. And my parents did own businesses, and I knew for the Laundromat and car wash, they had parts they had to purchase and machines and detergent. I just saw it as I'm starting a business, I'm going to need tools, I'm going to need these things, and I trust these women. So I got the smallest package because that's all I could do at that time. But I felt a lot of pressure to get more. And I was told . . . and now I see this is a huge red flag, but I didn't understand compensation or ranks or anything at this point yet. But I was also told the bigger package that you purchased, it'll put you in qualification for the first rank, which is a promotion and a pay raise."

A few months later Jennifer quit CPS and was investing in her future as an Arbonne representative. She says things went fast in the beginning. She was "hired" no questions asked; she began training immediately and buying all the products she could to familiarize herself with her new business. One of the first things she was told by her upline was to "Arbonnize" her life: switch out all of the products in her home for Arbonne equivalents. This meant all of her skin-care products and makeup, protein shakes and vitamins, hand soaps and lotions—everything around her house became Arbonne.

The manipulation didn't stop there. Jennifer says she was encouraged to do their patented cleanse, 30 Days to Healthy Living, which required her to drink two protein shakes a day and then have a "balanced meal," whatever that means. This is the exact same thing SlimFast pitches, but the similarities didn't occur to Jennifer at the time. Suddenly, she was talking about and thinking about weight loss, which didn't sit well with her but she was told it was all part of the plan for success, and Jennifer was, if nothing else, an excellent student, driven to success in whatever she was doing.

She was also told to each month throw eight Arbonne parties or get in front of forty new faces to grow her business. She began driving far from home to reach this goal, working nights and weekends (sound familiar?). But she did it. She started recruiting and using the same tactics on those recruits: telling them to buy the bigger starter package, to Arbonnize their homes, to aim for greatness and it would come. One of the most manipulative things Jennifer regrets doing what her upline taught her: tell your recruits they need four of every product on hand. One for their home, one to give to friends and family, one to sample at parties, and one just in case you run out. Arbonne sells hundreds of products, but let's just look at one, the face wash Jennifer first fell in love with. Today, in 2023, it's priced at $49 retail, but if you joined her team, you could buy it for just $39.20. Multiply that by four and that's $156.80 Jennifer just "earned" for her business on one product and one recruit. Things snowballed fast and she ranked up quickly following these sales tactics.

"I was teaching my team what I was taught. They talk about building a table as one of your first goals: you are one leg, and if you recruit three other people, then you have a table with four legs, and if they do the same . . . you see where this is going." I do, but Jennifer didn't at the time.

Soon, she was seeing paychecks of $2,000 to $3,000, but like all MLMers she wasn't doing a profit-and-loss statement, so though the numbers looked great, she had no idea what she was netting. "I had someone join my team who had been with another multi-level marketing company prior to joining Arbonne, and she had recognized that Arbonne miscalculated her paycheck. So I go to my upline who's supposed to be this Wall Street executive, this finance guru professional, and she's like, 'Oh, well, Arbonne will make it right, whatever it is.' And I'm like, 'Well, I would like to understand the compensation plan.' And she was like, 'Oh, don't worry. We plan on doing a whole training on that.' But what happens is, time goes by and you just forget about it."

So Jennifer's thinking she's making money, but that wasn't the only part that felt good. As she ranked up, she was being invited to speak at conferences (never mind she had to pay her way there). She became addicted to the attention, the "love bombing" as she refers to it. Her upline was calling her a rock star, her team was celebrating her promotions during every meeting, higher-ups were telling her she was destined for greatness. She just needed to achieve one last goal and she would be about as close to the top as she could get. If her team sold $40,000 of merchandise per month for three months, she would qualify for a white Arbonne-branded Mercedes. Jennifer put her head down and got to hustling.

Months one and two were not easy, but getting your team

to turn over that much volume three months in a row seemed impossible. But Jennifer got lucky. "That final month all of the new products got released, and this was actually one of the biggest product launches that Arbonne had had. The company told us, 'You're going to want the entire I Want It All set. You're going to want one set for yourself. You're going to want one set to give to your hostesses, people who have parties for you, to Christmas gifts for teachers, for day-care providers. You're going to want one set for your in-home presentations because you can't be using the set that you personally use, and then you're going to want one set as a backup because these products are going to sell out.' And so, I'm not kidding you, myself and several people on my team bought four sets." Jennifer recalls the price for one set to be somewhere around $500, making each recruit's purchase $2,000 for that month. She hit her goal and headed to the Mercedes dealership to pick up her car.

Now here's where things went sideways. She wasn't *given* a Mercedes. She and her husband had to apply for a loan using their own credit. She could choose the model, but it had to be white and it came with the Arbonne logo in chrome over the wheel wells. She had to pony up the down payment. The only thing Arbonne actually provided was a monthly bonus of exactly $800 toward her payment, but there was a catch: she could only get that bonus if her team continued to sell $40,000 a month. But, "you're also told how luxurious this is, and how this vehicle that you're driving around now, people are going to be asking you about your business. This is a recruitment tool. This is social proof. This is proof that the business works."

Except in a town of fifteen hundred people, it didn't. There was no one left to recruit. There was no one she knew whose house wasn't already Arbonnized. After eight years with the company, Jennifer was ready to give up. But she felt trapped. "I know unless people have gone through something like this, or maybe they've been with a narcissist or some situation where they realized the emperor wasn't wearing any clothes, they may not understand. If people quit and they weren't showing up on calls anymore, you would see upline leaders— and I even did this later on, too—but you would hear them say, 'Oh, so-and-so just quit. Her mindset's not really in the right place. She hasn't really been working on herself. I feel so bad for her.' You had pity for them, and I did that, too. Which is horrifying to admit, but it's true. I did the same thing to people."

Finally, in the spring of 2022, Jennifer left the company. She says she's still processing what happened to her, with new revelations coming to her each day about the ways she was manipulated, coerced, and ultimately ripped off. She still drives the Mercedes, though.

Epilogue

Over the past couple of years, the anti-MLM movement has been on a roll. There are support groups, podcasts, Reddit communities, and MLM-specific deprogrammers. But just as quickly as people catch on that one MLM is bad, that they've lost money to a corrupt scheme, a new one will pop up with a slightly different angle, a slightly different dazzling sell, and we're back to square one.

Lately I've been mesmerized by some TikTok accounts that, despite TikTok's supposed "no MLMs" rule, go live regularly. My "favorite" is this company called Bomb Party. They sell jewelry that's hidden inside bath bombs. People order a $20 bath bomb; the presenter plops it in water, chitchats with people who are watching, and, when it's done fizzing, fishes out what looks like wadded-up tinfoil. Slowly, the presenter unwraps it to reveal a plastic bag with a piece of paper in it and eventually finds a ring in there as well. Then the presenter reads the description of the ring while showing viewers a close-up, saying something like "This ring is called Her Majesty's Delight" or something stupider. Most rings contain cubic zirconias and lab-created gems in rhodium plating, whatever that is. Then, the presenter includes the manufacturer's suggested retail price, which is almost always over $100. That's the most annoying part, that people are paying $20 not only for a ring but for this person's time and for the bath bomb part and for shipping and so forth and then believing they've purchased something of much greater value. But that's because that's not what's happening.

What's happening is recruiting. Over and over the presenters tell those of us watching how we can join their team, how we can learn to do exactly what we're watching. Many of the presenters are doing the Bomb Parties while also yelling at their kids in the other room or demanding refills of water from off-camera spouses. Just today I watched a Bomb Party where the woman said that you can get in for just $99, but that kit doesn't contain enough jewelry to have a good online party, so she suggests starting with the kit closer to $600. She said the quiet part out loud: that you can get in for just $99 except you won't be able to earn any money on that. I keep watching though, it's actually kinda fun.

Acknowledgments

Let's get down to business first: I need to thank Laura Mayer for bringing us the opportunity to make the podcast that inspired this book, Dann Gallucci for all of his original reporting on the show and support over the years it took me to write this, Peter Clowney for his expert editing, and MacKenzie Kassab and Lyra Smith for helping produce that first season. My agent, Anthony Mattero at CAA, basically took a transcript of that season and helped shape it into a book proposal that my wonderful editor at Atria, Stephanie Hitchcock, took a liking to. Amazing. And to her assistant, Erica Siudzinski, for keeping track of so many loose ends throughout the process.

I had a lot of help writing and organizing this thing, which happened during the pandemic when we all had a million other worries. Thanks to my collaborator Brooke Carey for guiding me when I didn't think I knew what I was doing, and Jennifer

Swann, Riley Madincea, and Carolyn Lipka for their help with research. And to my sister Nancy Golombisky, who helped run our company and picked up the slack with the book and my child pretty much whenever I needed it. A true gem.

I need to thank all of my family here as well for their generous participation in making these stories come to life. Grandma Ruth and Aunt Amy, you two are some killer story-tellers and I love you both very much. My parents, who have always been supportive of my creative pursuits, even though I talk about dirty stuff all the time. My other siblings, Andy, Ginger, and Roberta, who just keep my heart full. And all my friends who sell MLMs and were willing to talk to me, you're the best (even though I wish you would quit!). To my original sources, most of whose names were changed, you are truly the center of these stories.

I also need to thank my giant and wonderfully supportive circle of friends who talked me out of impostor syndrome, listened as I whined about how hard this was, or just offered me an ear and hugs. There are too many of you to list, and for that I feel very, very #blessed.

And, Ira Glass, thank you for teaching me how to write stories that people might actually like.

Lastly, to my sweet daughter, Goldie: Thank you for giving me a reason to be here doing stuff. Even though I dedicated this book to Grandma Maxine, it's really for you. She's dead, she'll never know.

Notes

Chapter 1:
Anatomy of a Scheme

1   "Direct Selling Association Releases Data Showing Record High Sales and Customers in the U.S. in 2021" (press release), Direct Selling Association, June 7, 2022, https://www.dsa.org/events /news/individual-press-release/direct-selling-association-releases -data-showing-record-high-sales-and-customers-in-the-u.s. -in-2021.

2   "My Pure Romance Story: Nikki," Pure Romance, October 9, 2020, https://buzz.pureromance.com/2020/10/my-pure-romance-story -nikki/.

3   Jon M. Taylor, "The Case (for and) against Multi-level Marketing," Consumer Awareness Institute, 2011, 7–19, https://centerforin quiry.org/wp-content/uploads/sites/33/quackwatch/taylor.pdf.

4   *FTC v. Herbalife of Am., Inc.*, No. 2:16-cv-05217 (C.D. Cal. 2016), https://www.ftc.gov/enforcement/cases-proceedings/142-3037 /herbalife-international-america-inc-et-al.

5   Jen Wieczner, "Carl Icahn Says Herbalife Is Definitely Not a Pyra-
     mid Scheme," *Fortune*, July 18, 2016, https://www.yahoo.com/news
     /carl-icahn-says-herbalife-definitely-214424860.html.

6   Taylor, "Case."

7   Julie (pseudonym, former Pure Romance seller), interviewed by the
     author, July 22, 2021; and "Vibrators & Personal Massagers," Adam
     & Eve, accessed June 12, 2023, https://www.adameve.com/adult
     -sex-toys/vibrators-ch-1011.aspx.

8   "Hybrid Gel Lubricant," Pure Romance, accessed June 12, 2023,
     https://pureromance.com/products/hybrid-gel-lubricant.

9   "K-Y Jelly Personal Lubricant, 4 fl oz," Amazon, accessed June 12,
     2023, https://www.amazon.com/Personal-Lubricant-K-Y-Jelly-Water
     /dp/B00ZCMD9K4/.

10   Abby Vesoulis and Eliana Dockterman, "How MLM Distributors
     Are Using Coronavirus to Grow," *Time*, July 9, 2020, https://time
     .com/5864712/multilevel-marketing-schemes-coronavirus/.

Chapter 2:
Women's Work

1   Bridget Read, "Hey, Hun! In Women's Joblessness, Multi-level Mar-
     keters Saw Opportunity," The Cut, February 3, 2021, https://www
     .thecut.com/2021/02/pandemic-unemployment-multi-level-mar
     keting.html.

2   Michael J. Silverstein and Kate Sayre, "The Female Economy," *Har-
     vard Business Review*, September 2009, https://hbr.org/2009/09/the
     -female-economy.

3   Kim Parker, "Women More Than Men Adjust Their Careers for
     Family Life," Pew Research Center, October 1, 2015, https://www
     .pewresearch.org/short-reads/2015/10/01/women-more-than-men
     -adjust-their-careers-for-family-life/.

4   Ben Sira, Ecclesiasticus 26:29.

5   David H. McConnell Sr., *A History of the California Perfume Company* (New York, 1903), https://www.californiaperfumecompany.com/company/cal_great_oak.html.

6   Katina Manko, *Ding Dong! Avon Calling! The Women and Men of Avon Products, Incorporated* (New York: Oxford University Press, 2021).

7   McConnell, *California Perfume Company*.

8   Marylin Bender, "Avon: Chiming True?," *New York Times*, November 28, 1971, https://www.nytimes.com/1971/11/28/archives/avon-chiming-true-avon-chiming-true.html.

9   Vicky Flanders, "Persis Albee: The 1st Avon Lady," Historical Society of Cheshire County, New Hampshire, 2007, https://docplayer.net/40344038-Persis-albee-the-1-st-avon-lady-research-guide-biography-photographs-secondary-sources.html.

10 Ibid.

11 Carol H. Krismann, *Encyclopedia of American Women in Business: From Colonial Times to the Present* (Westport, CT: Greenwood Press, 2005), 19.

12 McConnell, *California Perfume Company*.

13 Manko, *Avon Calling!*, 139.

14 McConnell, *California Perfume Company*.

15 Manko, *Avon Calling!*, 166.

16 Ibid., 1.

17 Bob Kealing, *Life of the Party: The Remarkable Story of How Brownie Wise Built, and Lost, a Tupperware Party Empire* (New York: Crown Archetype, 2016).

18 Ibid.

19 Susan Freinkel, "A Brief History of Plastic's Conquest of the World," *Scientific American*, May 29, 2011, https://www.scientificamerican.com/article/a-brief-history-of-plastic-world-conquest/.

20 Kat Eschner, "The Story of Brownie Wise, the Ingenious Marketer behind the Tupperware Party," *Smithsonian Magazine*, April 10, 2018, https://www.smithsonianmag.com/smithsonian-in

stitution/story-brownie-wise-ingenious-marketer-behind-tupper
ware-party-180968658/.

21 Ibid.

22 Kealing, *Life of the Party*.

23 Ibid.

24 Ibid., 38.

25 Ibid., 75.

26 Laurie Kahn, dir., "Tupperware!," *American Experience*, season 16, episode 6, PBS, aired February 9, 2004, transcript at https://www -tc.pbs.org/wgbh/americanexperience/media/pdf/transcript/tupper ware_transcript.pdf.

27 Ibid.

28 Eschner, "Story of Brownie Wise."

29 Kahn, "Tupperware!"

30 Kealing, *Life of the Party*, 92.

31 "Become a Rep," Avon, accessed June 12, 2023, https://www.avon .com/becomearep.

32 "Start a Business," Amway, accessed June 12, 2023, https://www .amway.com/en_US/start-a-business.

33 "Become a Fashion Entrepreneur," LuLaRoe, accessed June 12, 2023, https://www.lularoe.com/join-lularoe.

Chapter 3:
Original Hucksters

1 Gordon H. Chang, *Fateful Ties: A History of America's Preoccupation with China* (Cambridge, MA: Harvard University Press, 2015), loc. 809, Kindle.

2 Ibid., loc. 872.

3 Sam Rehnborg, *The Nutrilite Story: Past, Present, Future* (Ada, MI: Amway, 2009), 35.

4 Ibid., 38.

5   Ibid., 56.

6   Dan Hurley, *Natural Causes: Death, Lies and Politics in America's Vitamin and Herbal Supplement Industry* (New York: Broadway Books, 2006), 38.

7   Catherine Price, *Vitamania: How Vitamins Revolutionized the Way We Think about Food* (New York: Penguin Books, 2016), 44.

8   Ibid., 88.

9   Carol Ballentine, "Sulfanilamide Disaster," *FDA Consumer Magazine*, June 1981, https://www.fda.gov/files/about%20fda/published/The-Sulfanilamide-Disaster.pdf.

10 Ibid.

11 "FDA History—Part II: 1938, Food, Drug, Cosmetic Act," Food and Drug Administration, accessed June 12, 2023, https://www.fda.gov/about-fda/changes-science-law-and-regulatory-authorities/part-ii-1938-food-drug-cosmetic-act.

12 "Notices of Judgement under the Federal Food, Drug, and Cosmetic Act, 3381–3383," Food and Drug Administration, issued August 1951, https://quackwatch.org/wp-content/uploads/sites/33/quackwatch/casewatch/fda/court/nutrilite.pdf.

13 Rehnborg, *Nutrilite Story*, 187.

14 Ibid., 248.

15 Kathryn A. Jones, *Amway Forever: The Amazing Story of a Global Business Phenomenon* (Hoboken, NJ: John Wiley & Sons, 1956), 40–41.

16 Lester L. Lev, "The Nutrilite Consent Decree," *Food, Drug, Cosmetic Law Journal* 7, no. 1 (January 1952): 56–69.

17 Peter Weber, "How the Vitamin Industrial Complex Swindled America," *The Week*, January 8, 2015, https://theweek.com/articles/454161/how-vitamin-industrial-complex-swindled-america.

18 Hazel K. Stiebeling, "Are We Well Fed? A Report on the Diets of Families in the United States," United States Department of Agriculture, Miscellaneous Publication No. 430, 1941, https://www.ars.usda.gov/ARSUserFiles/80400530/pdf/hist/bhe_1941_misc_pub_430.pdf.

19   "New Research Targets Previewed by Developer of Nutrilite Food Supplement!" (advertisement), *Life*, June 30, 1958, 108–9.

20   *Mytinger Casselberry, Inc. v. F.T.C.*, 301 F.2d 534 (D.C. Cir. 1962).

Chapter 4:
The American Way

1   Chase Peterson-Withorn, "Inside Betsy Devos' Billions: Just How Rich Is the Education Secretary?," *Forbes*, August 1, 2019, https://www.forbes.com/sites/chasewithorn/2019/07/24/inside-betsy-devos-billions-just-how-rich-is-the-education-secretary.

2   Leo Jakobson, "Diamonds Are Forever," Successful Meetings (website), December 7, 2009, https://www.successfulmeetings.com/Strategy/Meetings-Events/Diamonds-Are-Forever.

3   Jay Van Andel, *An Enterprising Life: An Autobiography* (New York: HarperBusiness, 1998), 2–3.

4   Kathryn A. Jones, *Amway Forever: The Amazing Story of a Global Business Phenomenon* (Hoboken, NJ: John Wiley & Sons, 1956), 18.

5   Ibid., 19.

6   Van Andel, *Enterprising Life*, 6–8.

7   Jones, *Amway Forever*, 38.

8   "Victor Views: The History Behind the Wolverine," University of Michigan, December 2017, https://campusinfo.umich.edu/article/victor-views-history-behind-wolverine.

9   Van Andel, *Enterprising Life*, 15.

10   Aaron M. Renn, "Manufacturing a Comeback," *City Journal*, March 23, 2023, https://www.city-journal.org/html/manufacturing-comeback-15833.html.

11   Van Andel, *Enterprising Life*, 19.

12   Ibid., 26.

13   Ibid., 35.

14   Jones, *Amway Forever*, 21.

15 Ibid., 23.

16 Ibid. 24.

17 Van Andel, *Enterprising Life*, 42.

18 Jones, *Amway Forever*, 23.

19 Van Andel, *Enterprising Life*, 57–60.

20 "In the Matter of Amway Corporation, Inc.," Federal Trade Commission, Docket 9023, 1975–1979, https://www.ftc.gov/sites/default/files/documents/commission_decision_volumes/volume-93/ftc_volume_decision_93_january_-_june_1979pages_618-738.pdf.

21 Jones, *Amway Forever*, 50.

22 Ibid., 50–52.

23 Ibid., 56.

24 "Supermarkets & Grocery Stores in the U.S.—Number of Businesses 2002–2028," IBISWorld, accessed June 12, 2023, https://www.ibisworld.com/industry-statistics/number-of-businesses/supermarkets-grocery-stores-united-states/.

25 Davor Mondom, "Compassionate Capitalism: Amway and the Role of Small-Business Conservatives in the New Right," in *Modern American History*, ed. Darren Dochuk and Sarah B. Snyder (New York: Cambridge University Press, 2018), 343–61.

26 Ibid., 355.

27 Richard M. DeVos and Charles Paul Conn, *Believe!* (New York: Pocket Books, 1976), 17.

28 "Join Us: Independent Consultant," Arbonne International, accessed June 12, 2023, https://www.arbonne.com/us/en/join-us/independent-consultant.

29 "Become a Brand Partner," Young Living Essential Oils, accessed June 12, 2023, https://www.youngliving.com/us/en/company/becoming-a-brand-partner.

30 "Join Us—Join the Community and Become a Fashion Entrepreneur," LuLaRoe, accessed June 12, 2023, https://www.lularoe.com/join-lularoe.

31 crappymlm (u/crappymlm), "The Girl Boss in Me Sees the Girl Boss in You, How Empowering," Reddit, August 9, 2021, https://www.reddit.com/r/Youniqueamua/comments/p1b0zd/the_girl_boss_in_me_sees_the_girl_boss_in_you_how/.

32 "Empowered You," dōTERRA Essential Oils, accessed June 12, 2023, https://www.doterra.com/US/en/empowered-you.

33 "Start Your Own Business by Becoming an Amway IBO: Make Money from Home," Amway, accessed June 12, 2023, https://www.amway.com/en_US/start-a-business.

34 "Affirmations for Success in Your Direct Sales Business," Jackie Ulmer, accessed June 12, 2023, https://jackieulmer.com/affirmations-for-success-in-your-direct-sales-business/.

35 "Lularoe Mark Stidham: 'You're Stale' and 'Wrestling with Pigs' Webinar—04182017" (video), posted on Lularoefail (website) by @lularoefail, February 12, 2018, 42:53, https://lularoefail.com/2018/02/12/lularoe-mark-stidham-youre-stale-wrestling-pigs-webinar-04182017/.

36 Brownie Wise, *Best Wishes, Brownie Wise: How to Put Your Wishes to Work* (Orlando, FL: Tupperware Corporation, 1957), 58.

Chapter 5:
Mind Games

1 R. C. Allen, *William Penn Patrick* (Chicago: Best Books, 1970), 9.

2 Sidney Katz, "Hung Jury: The Rosy World of Nutri-bio," *Maclean's*, July 28, 1962, https://archive.macleans.ca/article/1962/07/28/the-rosy-world-of-nutri-bio.

3 Katie Dowd, "The Incredible Implosion of the Bay Area's Biggest Pyramid Scheme," *SFGATE*, December 15, 2022, https://www.sfgate.com/sfhistory/article/The-incredible-implosion-of-Holiday-Magic-16785971.php.

4 Allen, *William Penn Patrick*, 16.

5   "A Not So Magical Holiday with Holiday Magic Cosmetics," The Makeup Museum (website), February 25, 2021, https://www.make upmuseum.org/home/2021/02/holiday-magic-cosmetics.html.

6   *In the Matter of Holiday Magic Inc.*, 84 FTC 748 (1974), https://www.mlmlegal.com/legal-cases/HolidayMagic_v_FTC1974.php.

7   *Holiday Magic, Inc. v. Warren*, 357 F. Supp. 20 (E.D. Wis. 1973).

8   Ibid.

9   Ibid.

10 Matt Novak, "The Untold Story of Napoleon Hill, the Greatest Self-Help Scammer of All Time," *Gizmodo*, December 6, 2016, https://gizmodo.com/the-untold-story-of-napoleon-hill-the-greatest -self-he-1789385645.

11 Napoleon Hill, *Think and Grow Rich* (paperback) (New York: TarcherPerigee, 2005). Amazon, https://www.amazon.com/Think -Grow-Rich-Landmark-Bestseller/dp/1585424331.

12 Gene Church and Conrad D. Carnes, *The Pit: A Group Encounter Defiled* (New York: Pocket Books, 1973), 13–25.

13 Ibid., 136–44.

14 Wallace Turner, "Lawsuits Threaten Millionaire Promoter of Pyramid Sales," *New York Times*, February 19, 1973, https://www .nytimes.com/1973/02/19/archives/lawsuits-threaten-millionaire -promoter-ofpyramid-sales-states-have.html.

15 Ibid.

16 Carla Correa, "A Timeline of the Nxivm Sex Cult Case," *New York Times*, September 8, 2021, https://www.nytimes.com/article/nxivm -timeline.html.

17 Ibid.

18 Frank Parlato, "13 Raniere Quotes: Words of a Compassionate Teacher!," Frank Report (website), January 31, 2016, https://frankreport.com/2016/01/30/13-raniere-quotes-words-of-compassionate-teacher-if-he-practices-what-he-preaches/.

19 Minyvonne Burke, "NXIVM Co-founder Nancy Salzman Sentenced to 3.5 years in Prison," NBC News, September 8, 2021,

https://www.nbcnews.com/news/us-news/nxivm-co-founder
-nancy-salzman-sentenced-3-5-years-prison-n1278702.

20 DōTERRA Essential Oils USA (@dōTERRA), "How Do You Leave
Behind Limiting Thoughts?," Instagram video, January 18, 2022,
https://www.instagram.com/p/CY4RAneB7uY/.

21 Jeunesse Global Instagram, accessed June 12, 2023, https://www
.instagram.com/jeunesseglobal/.

22 "Richest 1% Bag Nearly Twice as Much Wealth as the Rest of the
World Put Together over the Past Two Years" (press release), Oxfam
International, January 16, 2023, https://www.oxfam.org/en/press
-releases/richest-1-bag-nearly-twice-much-wealth-rest-world-put
-together-over-past-two-years.

Chapter 6:
The Watchmen

1 John Frasca, *Con Man or Saint?* (Anderson, SC: Droke House; dis-
tributed by Grosset & Dunlap, New York, 1969), 80.

2 "Turner Decrees a Xanadu in Florida," *New York Times*, June 16,
1973, https://www.nytimes.com/1973/06/16/archives/turner-decrees
-a-xanadu-in-florida-additions-planned-a-pleasure.html.

3 Ibid.

4 Michael C. Jensen, "S.E.C. Lays Fraud to Holiday Magic," *New
York Times*, June 29, 1973, https://www.nytimes.com/1973/06/29
/archives/sec-lays-fraud-to-holiday-magic-investors-said-to-have
-been-cheated.html.

5 "Holiday Magic Explained," Explained Today (website), accessed
June 12, 2023, http://everything.explained.today/Holiday_Magic/.

6 *Holiday Magic, Inc. v. Warren*, 357 F. Supp. 20 (E.D. Wis. 1973).

7 William F. Rawson, "2 Sentenced in Scheme to Bilk Investors,"
Washington Post, August 21, 1987, https://www.washingtonpost

.com/archive/business/1987/08/21/2-sentenced-in-scheme-to-bilk
-investors/cfe6c727-36d1-4eae-b9f3-42002b284bba/.

8 Dan Morgan, "Selling Free Enterprise," *Washington Post*, March 14, 1981, https://www.washingtonpost.com/archive/politics/1981/03/14/selling-free-enterprise/951e73a4-c888-48f9-8726-ddc31d15b471/.

9 Dale Russakoff and Juan Williams, "Rearranging 'Amway Event' for Reagan," *Washington Post*, January 22, 1984, https://www.washingtonpost.com/archive/politics/1984/01/22/rearranging-amway-event-for-reagan/b3e74482-5ce0-4d20-9f98-ebdc9b4d4918/.

10 Davor Mondom, "Compassionate Capitalism: Amway and the Role of Small-Business Conservatives in the New Right," in *Modern American History*, ed. Darren Dochuk and Sarah B. Snyder (New York: Cambridge University Press, 2018).

11 Ibid., 355.

12 "*Forbes* Profile: Van Andel Family," *Forbes*, July 1, 2015, https://www.forbes.com/profile/van-andel/.

13 Benjamin Stupples, "DeVos Heir to $5 Billion Amway Fortune Bets on Family Office," *Bloomberg*, February 9, 2022, https://www.bloomberg.com/news/articles/2022-02-09/devos-heir-to-5-billion-amway-fortune-bets-on-family-office.

Chapter 7:
From Prophets to Profiteers

1 Federal Trade Commission, "Warning Regarding Health and Earnings Claims Related to Coronavirus Disease 2019 (COVID-19)" (email to dōTERRA International), April 24, 2020, https://www.ftc.gov/system/files/warning-letters/covid-19-letter_to_doterra_international_llc.pdf.

2 Food and Drug Administration to dōTERRA International, LLC, September 22, 2014, https://wayback.archive-it.org/7993

/20191212082653/https:/www.fda.gov/inspections-compliance
-enforcement-and-criminal-investigations/warning-letters/doterra
-international-llc-09222014.

3 Lori Wilson, "Warning: Georgia Poison Center Warns about Using
Essential Oils around Kids, Pets," WSB-TV, June 14, 2019, https://
www.wsbtv.com/news/2-investigates/warning-georgia-poison-center
-warns-about-using-essential-oils-around-kids-pets/958237578/.

4 "Veggie Caps: dōTERRA Essential Oils," dōTERRA Essential Oils,
accessed June 12, 2023, https://www.doterra.com/US/en/p/usage
-internal-veggie-caps.

5 FTC, "Warning" email to dōTERRA.

6 Ibid.

7 Joseph Charles Maroon and Jeffrey W. Bost, "Omega-3 Fatty Acids
(Fish Oil) as an Anti-inflammatory: An Alternative to Nonsteroidal
Anti-inflammatory Drugs for Discogenic Pain," *Surgical Neurology*
65, no. 4 (April 2006): 326–31, https://pubmed.ncbi.nlm.nih.gov
/16531187/.

8 Matthew P. Mayo, *Hornswogglers, Fourflushers & Snake-Oil Salesmen: True Tales of the Old West's Sleaziest Swindlers* (Guilford, CT:
TwoDot, 2015), 55.

9 "Clark Stanley's Snake Oil Liniment," National Museum of American History (website), accessed June 27, 2023, https://americanhis
tory.si.edu/collections/search/object/nmah_1298331.

10 Mayo, *Hornswogglers*, 59.

11 Kiona N. Smith, "6 Weird Ways People Tried to Cure the 1918 Influenza," *Forbes*, February 28, 2021, https://www.forbes.com/sites
/kionasmith/2021/02/28/6-weird-ways-people-tried-to-cure-the
-1918-influenza/?sh=1854548198a5.

12 Teri Shors and Eric Stanelle, "Influenza Medicines, Then and Now,"
University of Wisconsin Oshkosh, accessed June 12, 2023, http://
www.uwosh.edu/oldarchives/flu/response2.htm.

13 Sabrina Stierwalt, "Do Essential Oils Work? Here's What Science
Says," *Scientific American*, March 7, 2020, https://www.scientific

american.com/article/do-essential-oils-work-heres-what-science
-says/.

14 "Business Guidance Concerning Multi-Level Marketing," Federal
Trade Commission, accessed June 12, 2023, https://www.ftc.gov
/business-guidance/resources/business-guidance-concerning-multi
-level-marketing.

15 Lauren Kutschke, "The Proper Way to Do a Master Lemon Detox,"
Live Infinitely (website), accessed June 12, 2023, https://www
.liveinfinitely.com/pages/the-proper-way-to-do-a-master-lemon
-detox.

16 Tim Hanson, "Man Arrested on Medical Charges," *Spokane (WA)
Spokesman-Review*, May 9, 1983.

17 Ibid.

18 Eva F. Briggs, "A Critical Look at Gary Young, Young Living Essential Oils, and Raindrop Therapy," circulated online 2002, https:
//www.sequenceinc.com/fraudfiles/wp-content/uploads/2015/03
/gary-young-living-essential-oils.pdf.

19 Hanson, "Man Arrested."

20 " 'Patient' Submits Blood (from Cat), Is Given Diagnosis," *Los Angeles Times*, October 23, 1987, https://www.latimes.com/archives
/la-xpm-1987-10-23-mn-10747-story.html.

21 Rachel Monroe, "How Essential Oils Became the Cure for Our Age
of Anxiety," *New Yorker*, October 9, 2017, https://www.newyorker
.com/magazine/2017/10/09/how-essential-oils-became-the-cure
-for-our-age-of-anxiety.

22 "Case #13-2020—Challenge—Young Living Essential Oils, LCC,"
BBB National Programs, accessed June 27, 2023, https://bbbpro
grams.org/programs/all-programs/dssrc/ccd/case-13-2020-chal
lenge-young-living-essential-oils-llc.

23 "Young Living Named to Top 10 of Direct Selling News Global
100 List," PR Newswire (website), April 23, 2021, https:.//www
.prnewswire.com/news-releases/young-living-named-to-top-10-of
-direct-selling-news-global-100-list-301276114.html.

24 *Young Living Essential Oils v. dōTERRA International*, No.2:2013 cv00502 (D. Utah 2013).

25 Monroe, "How Essential Oils Became the Cure."

26 "FTC Sends Second Round of Warning Letters to Multi-level Marketers Regarding Coronavirus Related Health and Earnings Claims" (press release), Federal Trade Commission, June 5, 2020, https://www.ftc.gov/news-events/news/press-releases/2020/06/ftc-sends-second-round-warning-letters-multi-level-marketers-regarding-coronavirus-related-health.

27 "Multi-level Marketer AdvoCare Will Pay $150 Million to Settle FTC Charges It Operated an Illegal Pyramid Scheme" (press release), Federal Trade Commission, October 2, 2019, https://www.ftc.gov/news-events/news/press-releases/2019/10/multi-level-marketer-advocare-will-pay-150-million-settle-ftc-charges-it-operated-illegal-pyramid.

28 *FTC v. Herbalife of Am., Inc.*, No. 2:16-cv-05217 (C.D. Cal. 2016), https://www.ftc.gov/enforcement/cases-proceedings/142-3037/herbalife-international-america-inc-et-al.

29 "Herbalife Net Worth 2010–2023," Macrotrends, accessed June 12, 2023, https://www.macrotrends.net/stocks/charts/HLF/herbalife/net-worth.

Chapter 8:
Women's Work Redux

1 "About Younique," Younique, accessed June 12, 2023, https://www.youniqueproducts.com/business/about.

2 Sharon Terlep and Patrick Thomas, "Coty Ends Partnership with Younique," *Wall Street Journal*, August 28, 2019, https://www.wsj.com/articles/coty-ends-partnership-with-younique-11567000290.

3 Amy McCarthy, "The Rabidly Followed Leggings Brand You Can Only Buy on Facebook," Racked, June 16, 2016, https://www

.racked.com/2016/6/16/11898266/lularoe-leggings-facebook
-multi-level-marketing.

4   Gina Tron, "Who Are Multi-Level Marketing Company LuLaRoe
     Creators Mark Stidham and DeAnne Brady?," Oxygen, Septem-
     ber 9, 2021, https://www.oxygen.com/true-crime-buzz/who-are
     -mark-stidham-and-deanne-brady.

5   Áine Cain, "LuLaRoe's Founder Celebrated Her Birthday with a
     Lavish Masquerade Party Complete with Acrobatic Dancers and
     Cardboard Caricatures of Her Face While the Company Faces Mul-
     tiple Lawsuits," *Business Insider*, January 29, 2019, https://www
     .businessinsider.com/lularoe-deanne-stidham-masquerade-party
     -2019-1.

6   R. Thayne Robson, "Wealth, Attitudes Towards," in *Encyclopedia of
     Mormonism*, ed. Daniel H. Ludlow (New York: Macmillan, 1992),
     1551.

7   Kirsten Fleming, "How LuLaRoe Cost Some Women Their Homes,
     Cars, Savings, and Marriages," *New York Post*, September 18, 2021,
     https://nypost.com/2021/09/18/lularoe-cost-some-women-their
     -homes-savings-and-marriages/.

8   Shelby Heinrick, "28 Facts from the 'Rise and Fall of LuLaRoe'
     Documentary That Prove It's One of the Darkest MLMs Out
     There," *Buzzfeed*, December 31, 2021, https://www.buzzfeed.com
     /shelbyheinrich/lularoe-documentary-facts.

9   Ibid.

10   Hayley Peterson, "One of LuLaRoe's Most Iconic Executives Has
     Suddenly Left as Some Ex-sellers Claim the Company Owes Them
     Thousands of Dollars in Refunds," *Business Insider*, October 8,
     2018, https://www.businessinsider.com/lularoes-patrick-winget-exits
     -company-amid-refund-complaints-2018-10.

11   Associated Press, "$1B Suit Claims LuLaRoe Encouraged Women
     to Sell Breast Milk for Inventory," *New York Post*, October 27, 2017,
     https://nypost.com/2017/10/27/1b-suit-claims-lularoe-encouraged
     -women-to-sell-breast-milk-for-inventory/.

12 Maurine Startup and Elbert Startup, *The Secret Power of Femininity* (San Gabriel, CA: American Family and Femininity Institute, 1969), viii.

13 Martha Weinman Lear, "The Second Feminist Wave," *New York Times*, March 10, 1968, https://www.nytimes.com/1968/03/10/archives/the-second-feminist-wave.html.

14 Virginia Lee Warren, "New Lift for Old-Fashioned Femininity," *New York Times*, August 6, 1972, https://www.nytimes.com/1972/08/06/archives/new-lift-for-oldfashioned-femininity.html.

15 Áine Cain, "Inside the Life of LuLaRoe's Controversial Founder," *Business Insider*, October 3, 2019, https://www.businessinsider.com/lularoe-founder-deanne-stidham-life-2019-10.

16 Startup and Startup, *Secret Power*, x.

17 Ibid., xi.

18 Ibid., 101.

19 "*State of Washington v LuLaRoe*—Deanne Brady (Stidham) Deposition 8/8" (video), YouTube, posted by LLR Defective, October 7, 2021, 44:21, https://www.youtube.com/watch?v=ke1409q0S80.

20 Startup and Startup, *Secret Power*, 150.

21 Ibid., 153.

22 Ibid., 101.

23 "The Husband Unawareness Plan," MaryKayVictims.com, accessed June 12, 2023, https://marykayvictims.com/predatory-tactics/the-husband-unawareness-plan/.

24 Joey Keogh, "Is LuLaRoe Still in Business?," *The List*, January 12, 2022, https://www.thelist.com/731732/is-lularoe-still-in-business/.

25 Startup and Startup, *Secret Power*, 228–29.

26 Marinda Risk, "Utah MLM Explosion," *Daily Universe* (BYU), May 15, 2018, https://universe.byu.edu/2018/05/15/utah-shows-more-multi-level-marketing-activity-than-any-other-state-1/.

27 Utah Code, Title 76, Chapter 6a—"Pyramid Scheme Act," https://le.utah.gov/xcode/Title76/Chapter6a/C76-6a_1800001011800101.pdf.

28 Robert L. Fitzpatrick, "Utah Legislature Passes Pyramid Scheme 'Safe Harbor' Amendments," QuackWatch.org, March 1, 2006, https://quackwatch.org/mlm/legal/utahbill/.

29 "Is Utah the Fraud Capital of the U.S.?," Utah Office of the Attorney General (official website), accessed June 27, 2023, https://attorneygeneral.utah.gov/utah-fraud-capital/.

30 David A. Vise, "Fraud Seen Rampant in Utah," *Washington Post*, December 25, 1984, https://www.washingtonpost.com/archive/business/1984/12/25/fraud-seen-rampant-in-utah/6a2a1f23-687c-4175-b666-ffd31f0cbd30/.

Chapter 9:
Fool Me Twice

1 "Consumer Reports Articles," *Amway: The Untold Story* (blog), accessed June 27, 2023, https://www.cs.cmu.edu/~dst/Amway/AUS/cr.htm.

2 "Amway Home Automatic Dish Tablets," Amway, accessed June 12, 2023, https://www.amway.com/en_US/Amway-Home%E2%84%A2-Automatic-Dish-Tablets-p-109867.

3 "Cascade Complete Dishwasher Pods, 78 Count," Amazon, accessed June 12, 2023, https://www.amazon.com/Cascade-Complete-ActionPacs-Dishwasher-Detergent/dp/B01NCJSM2T.

4 "Amway Home All Fabric Bleach," Amway, accessed June 12, 2023, https://www.amway.com/en_US/Amway-Home%E2%84%A2-All-Fabric-Bleach-p-117774.

5 "OxiClean Versatile Stain Remover Powder, 5lbs," Amazon, accessed June 12, 2023, https://www.amazon.com/OxiClean-Versatile-Stain-Remover-Powder/dp/B00I8YAT42.

6 "Stop the Amway Tool Scam: Introduction, Our Story, and Website Orientation," Stop the Amway Tool Scam (website), accessed June 12, 2023, https://stoptheamwaytoolscam.wordpress.com/introduction/.

7   "Direct Selling in the United States: 2021 Industry Overview," Direct Selling Association, accessed June 12, 2023, https://www.dsa .org/statistics-insights/factsheets.

8   "What Is Multilevel Marketing (MLM)?," American Association of Retired Persons Foundation, accessed June 12, 2023, https://www .aarp.org/aarp-foundation/our-work/income/multilevel-marketing/.

9   Emma Penrod, "As the COVID-19 Economic Crisis Deepens, Financially Risky MLMs Are Moving In to Fill the Employment Void," *Business Insider*, July 14, 2020, https://www.insider.com/un employed-people-turn-to-risky-multi-level-marketing-companies -2020-7.

10 Herb Greenberg, "Multi-level Marketing Critic: Beware 'Main Street Bubble,'" CNBC, January 9, 2013, https://www.cnbc.com /id/100366687.

11 Eyal Zamir and Doron Teichman, "Mathematics, Psychology, and Law: The Legal Ramifications of the Exponential Growth Bias," Hebrew University of Jerusalem, Legal Research Paper No. 21-11, 2021, https://papers.ssrn.com/sol3/papers.cfm?abstract_id =3804329.

12 Robert Farrington, "Would You Rather Have a Penny That Doubles Each Day for a Month or $1 Million?," The College Investor, May 31, 2023, https://thecollegeinvestor.com/17145 /would-you-rather-have-a-penny-that-doubles-each-day-for-a -month-or-1-million/.

13 Randy Alcorn, "The Benefits and Pitfalls of Multilevel Marketing in the Christian Community," Eternal Perspective Ministries, February 25, 2019, https://www.epm.org/blog/2019/Feb/25/multilevel -marketing.

14 "Amway Business Reference Guide," Amway, accessed June 12, 2023, https://www.amway.com/medias/AmwayBusinessReference Guide-USEN.pdf.pdf?context=bWFzdGVyfHBkZnwxMjY1O DcxfGFwcGxpY2F0aW9uL3BkZnxwZGYvaDI4L2gzMi85NDkw

MDE4MDA5MTE4LnBkZnw2MTE4ZGU4YTI4MjFjNjJjM
jAyY2EzNWY1YjJlMzMyZDMxODBmMjE2NTM0ODZ
mMDM1YjkwYTJmMTgzNTUzNDA2.

15 "Steven Hassan's BITE Model of Authoritarian Control," Freedom
    of Mind Resource Center, accessed June 12, 2023, https://freedom
    ofmind.com/cult-mind-control/bite-model/.

16 Sara Silverstein, Jennifer Lee, and Amelia Kosciulek, "People Who
    Sell for Multilevel Marketing Companies Look Wildly Successful
    on Facebook, but the Reality Is Much More Complicated," *Business
    Insider*, August 6, 2019, https://www.insider.com/mlms-use-social
    -media-facebook-portray-financial-success-2019-7.

17 Stacie A. Bosley et al., "Decision-Making and Vulnerability in a
    Pyramid Scheme Fraud," *Journal of Behavioral and Experimental
    Economics* 80 (2019): 1–13, https://www.sciencedirect.com/science
    /article/pii/S2214804318304427.

Chapter 10:
Why Isn't Anyone Doing Anything?

1 "Who We Are," Direct Selling Association, accessed June 12, 2023,
   https://www.dsa.org/about/association.

2 Diane Bartz, "Biden Seeks 11% Jump in FTC Funding as Big
   Tech Cases Loom," Reuters, May 28, 2021, https://www.reuters
   .com/technology/biden-seeks-11-jump-ftc-funding-big-tech-cases
   -loom-2021-05-28/.

3 John Breyault (vice president of public policy, telecommunications,
   and fraud at National Consumers League), interviewed by the author, December 13, 2022.

4 "Global 100 Lists: Top Direct Selling Companies in the World—
   2023," *Direct Selling News*, accessed June 13, 2023, https://www
   .directsellingnews.com/global-100-lists/.

5   Jon M. Taylor, "The Case (for and) against Multi-level Marketing," Consumer Awareness Institute, 2011, https://centerforinquiry.org/wp-content/uploads/sites/33/quackwatch/taylor.pdf.

6   William Keep, "The Federal Trade Commission and Multi-level Marketing: Connecting the Dots," Seeking Alpha (website), October 21, 2020, https://seekingalpha.com/article/4380462-federal-trade-commission-and-multi-level-marketing-connecting-dots.

7   "Herbalife Reports Record Full Year 2016 Worldwide Volume" (press release), Herbalife, February 23, 2017, https://ir.herbalife.com/news-events/press-releases/detail/189/herbalife-reports-record-full-year-2016-worldwide-volume.

8   "FTC Sends Checks to Nearly 350,000 Victims of Herbalife's Multi-level Marketing Scheme" (press release), Federal Trade Commission, January 10, 2017, https://www.ftc.gov/news-events/news/press-releases/2017/01/ftc-sends-checks-nearly-350000-victims-herbalifes-multi-level-marketing-scheme.

9   "Herbalife Will Restructure Its Multi-level Marketing Operations and Pay $200 Million for Consumer Redress to Settle FTC Charges" (press release), Federal Trade Commission, July 15, 2016, https://www.ftc.gov/news-events/news/press-releases/2016/07/herbalife-will-restructure-its-multi-level-marketing-operations-pay-200-million-consumer-redress.

10 "Herbalife Nutrition Announces Full Year Record Results for the Second Consecutive Year," *Business Wire*, February 23, 2022, https://www.businesswire.com/news/home/20220223005444/en/Herbalife-Nutrition-Announces-Full-Year-Record-Results-for-the-Second-Consecutive-Year.

11 Dale Russakoff and Juan Williams, "Rearranging 'Amway Event' for Reagan," *Washington Post*, January 22, 1984, https://www.washingtonpost.com/archive/politics/1984/01/22/rearranging-amway-event-for-reagan/b3e74482-5ce0-4d20-9f98-ebdc9b4d4918/.

12 Ibid.

13 Ibid.

14 Andy Kroll, "Meet the New Kochs: The DeVos Clan's Plan to Defund the Left," *Mother Jones*, January/February 2014, https://www.mother jones.com/politics/2014/01/devos-michigan-labor-politics-gop/.

15 Russakoff and Williams, "Rearranging 'Amway Event.'"

16 Jeff Smith, "AIDS and Activism Part II: Reagan, DeVos and the 1980s Crisis," Grand Rapid Institute for Information Democracy, November 27, 2012, https://griid.org/2012/11/27/aids-and-activism-part-ii-reagan-devos-and-the-1980s-crisis/.

17 Ruth Marcus, "Bush to Get $100,000 for Amway Convention Speech," *Washington Post*, September 4, 1993, https://www.washingtonpost.com/archive/politics/1993/09/04/bush-to-get-100000-for-amway-convention-speech/f1d22921-e34c-4998-abef-c6358a111bce/.

18 Michelle Celarier, "Madeline Albright Is Freaking Out over Her Role as Herbalife Cheerleader," *New York Post*, April 17, 2014, https://nypost.com/2014/04/17/ex-secretary-of-state-albright-sweats-herbalife-ties/.

19 Robert L. FitzPatrick to President Barack Obama and Appropriate Members of Congress Overseeing the Federal Trade Commission and Consumer Financial Protection Bureau, October 7, 2010, https://archive.org/details/TheMainStreetBubbleAWhistleBlowers GuideToBusinessOpportunityFraud/page/n3/mode/1up.

20 Emily Stewart, "MLMs Might Not Be Able to Get Away with Their Shady Promises Much Longer," *Vox*, October 22, 2021, https://www.vox.com/the-goods/22732586/ftc-mlm-rohit-chopra-business-opportunity-rule.

21 Helaine Olen, "The Get-Rich-Quick Schemers Who Love the GOP," *Slate*, October 11, 2015, https://slate.com/business/2015/10/trump-carson-bush-all-benefited-from-multilevel-marketing-schemes.html.

22 Jessica Pressler, "'If I Can't Trust Donald Trump, Who Can I Trust?,'" *New York*, January 21, 2011, https://nymag.com/news/business/70831/.

23 Yelena Dzhanova, "Inside Trump's Ties to the Multi-level Marketing

Company That Gave Him $8.8 Million When He Was Approaching Financial Ruin," *Business Insider*, October 21, 2020, https://www.businessinsider.com/trump-relationship-acn-mlm-company-lawsuit-2020-10.

24 Craig Mauger, "DeVos Family Has Made at Least $82 Million in Political Contributions since 1999, according to Campaign Finance Disclosures," Michigan Campaign Finance Network, January 12, 2023, https://mcfn.org/node/6178/devos-family-has-made-at-least-82-million-in-political-contributions-since-1999-according-to-campaign-finance-disclosures.

25 Robert L. FitzPatrick, "Have I Got a Deal for You: The Endless Chain Offer," PyramidSchemeAlert (website), October 18, 2022, https://www.pyramidschemealert.org/have-i-got-a-deal-for-you-the-endless-chain-offer/.

26 Jeffrey Babener, "MLM Laws in 50 States," MLM Legal (website), accessed June 12, 2023, https://mlmlegal.com/statutes.html.

27 "LuLaRoe to Pay $4.75 Million to Resolve AG Ferguson's Lawsuit over Pyramid Scheme" (press release), Office of the Attorney General—Washington State, February 2, 2021, https://www.atg.wa.gov/news/news-releases/lularoe-pay-475-million-resolve-ag-ferguson-s-lawsuit-over-pyramid-scheme.

28 Amanda Garrity, "Is LuLaRoe Still in Business?," *Good Housekeeping*, September 18, 2021, https://www.goodhousekeeping.com/life/entertainment/a37638754/is-lularoe-still-in-business/.

29 Alexander Nazaryan, "Why Did Kamala Harris Let Herbalife off the Hook?," Yahoo! News, March 18, 2019, https://www.yahoo.com/now/kamala-harris-herbalife-accused-of-exploiting-latinos-090000896.html.

30 Kate Kelly, "How Does Harris View Big Business?," *New York Times*, October 30, 2020, https://www.nytimes.com/2020/10/30/business/kamala-harris-california-business.html.

31 "2022: Year in Review," Direct Selling Association, accessed June 12,

2023, https://www.dsa.org/docs/default-source/default/2022-year -in-review.pdf?sfvrsn=ccfcd4a5_2.

32 "2017–2021 Pyramid Scheme Class Action," Truth in Advertising, February 10, 2022, https://truthinadvertising.org/articles /2017-pyramid-scheme-lawsuits-chart/.

33 Robert L. FitzPatrick, "The Importance and Futility of Class Action Lawsuits against MLMs," PyramidSchemeAlert (website), May 1, 2019, https://www.pyramidschemealert.org/the-importance-and -futility-of-class-action-lawsuits-against-mlms/.

34 "Statement of Commissioner Rohit Chopra regarding the Business Opportunity Rule" (public statement), Federal Trade Commission, June 14, 2021, https://www.ftc.gov/system/files/documents/public _statements/1591046/statement_of_commissioner_rohit_chopra _regarding_the_business_opportunity_rule.pdf.

35 "FTC Shuts Down Credit Repair Pyramid Scheme Financial Education Services, Which Bilked More Than $213 Million from Consumers" (press release), Federal Trade Commission, May 31, 2022, https://www.ftc.gov/news-events/news/press-releases/2022/05 /ftc-shuts-down-credit-repair-pyramid-scheme-financial-education -services-which-bilked-more-213.

36 "FTC Warn Almost 700 Marketing Companies That They Could Face Civil Penalties If They Can't Back Up Their Product Claims" (press release), Federal Trade Commission, April 13, 2023, https: //www.ftc.gov/news-events/news/press-releases/2023/04/ftc-warns -almost-700-marketing-companies-they-could-face-civil-penalties -if-they-cant-back-their.

37 "Dissenting Statement of Commissioner Christine S. Wilson regarding the Issuance of a Notice of Penalty Offenses on Substantiation of Product Claims" (public statement), Federal Trade Commission, March 31, 2023, https://www.ftc.gov/legal-library /browse/cases-proceedings/public-statements/dissenting-statement -commissioner-christine-s-wilson-substantiation.

Index

About the Author

Jane Marie is a Peabody and Emmy Award–winning journalist, a former producer of *This American Life*, and the host of the podcasts *The Dream* and *DTR*. Her writing has appeared in *Jezebel*, *Cosmopolitan*, and more. She lives in Los Angeles with her daughter. Follow her on Twitter @SeeJaneMarie.